THE 12-HOUR MBA PROGRAM

The Key Concepts and Techniques in a Fraction of the Time

MILO SOBEL

PRENTICE HALL
Englewood Cliffs, New Jersey 07632

Library of Congress Cataloging-in-Publication Data

Sobel, Milo.
    The 12-hour MBA program / Milo Sobel.
      p. cm.
    Includes bibliographical reference and index.
    ISBN 0-13-097916-3—ISBN 0-13-045352-8 (pbk.)
    1. Industrial management.   I. Title.   II. Title: Twelve hour
MBA program.
    HD30.3.S63   1994   93-5832
    658—dc20   CIP

Printed in the United States of America

10 9 8 7 6

ISBN 0-13-097916-3   ISBN 0-13-045352-8(PBK)

ATTENTION: CORPORATIONS AND SCHOOLS

Prentice Hall books are available at quantity discounts with bulk purchase for educational,
business, or sales promotional use. For information, please write to: Prentice Hall Career &
Personal Development Special Sales, 113 Sylvan Avenue, Englewood Cliffs, NJ 07632. Please
supply: title of book, ISBN number, quantity, how the book will be used, date needed.

PRENTICE HALL
Career & Personal Development
Englewood Cliffs, NJ 07632
A Simon & Schuster Company

On the World Wide Web at http://www.phdirect.com

Prentice-Hall International (UK) Limited, *London*
Prentice-Hall of Australia Pty. Limited, *Sydney*
Prentice-Hall Canada Inc., *Toronto*
Prentice-Hall Hispanoamericana, S.A., *Mexico*
Prentice-Hall of India Private Limited, *New Delhi*
Prentice-Hall of Japan, Inc., *Tokyo*
Simon & Schuster Asia Pte. Ltd., *Singapore*
Editora Prentice-Hall do Brasil, Ltda., *Rio de Janeiro*

This book is dedicated to my parents,
Fay and Henry L. Sobel, MBAs
(My Beloved Allies)

ACKNOWLEDGMENTS

I wish to express my deep gratitude to the following individuals for their sage counsel and their contributions to this book:

From Academia:

Dr. Robert L. Crain, Professor of Education, Columbia University (Teachers College);

Dr. Geoffrey Moss, Lecturer in the Department of Management, American University;

Dr. I. Robert Parket, Professor of Marketing, City University of New York (Baruch College); and

Dr. Howard N. Ross, Professor of Economics and Finance and Academic Director of the Executive MBA Program, City University of New York (Baruch College).

From Industry:

Ms. Ayda Akbelen, Vice President of Career Services, Citicorp;

Ms. Gloria Gordon, Vice President of Technology Management, Xerox Corporation;

Dr. Howard S. Mase, Vice President of Human Resources, Metropolitan Life Insurance Company; and

Mr. Gary M. Zelamsky, Vice President of Operations, Viacom Cable.

From Prentice-Hall:

Mr. Glenn Shapiro, President of the Bureau of Business Practice, for his vision and commitment to this project; and

Mr. Drew Dreeland, editor extraordinaire, and Eve Mossman, production editor, for the invaluable insights that helped me to transform MBA IN A NUTSHELL® from seminar to book.

From the New York Institute of Finance:

Mr. Robert W. Gulick, President, Mr. William A. Rini, Senior Vice President, and Ms. Eunice Salton, Vice President, for their encouragement and cooperation.

From the Securities Operations Forum:

Ms. Susan Solomon, Vice President, for championing my cause in the early hours.

From my personal support team:

M. William Krasilovsky, Esq., legal eagle, for his advice, ethical and jurisprudential.

PROLOGUE: ORIENTATION TO THE PROGRAM

In 1986, I created MBA IN A NUT-SHELL,* an educational program designed to impart the distilled essence of the MBA curriculum in just two days. The program has since been presented for major corporations and in public seminars from coast to coast throughout the United States and Canada. The course was inspired by two seemingly unrelated influences: the accelerated pace of learning employed by the U.S. military's Officer Candidate School (which was created to transform enlisted personnel into officers within a 90-day time frame, rather than the four years required by West Point and Annapolis) and by the anecdotal reports of MBA alumni that less than 10 percent of their graduate business school curriculum is actually necessary and useful in their careers. *MBA IN A NUTSHELL* promised

*MBA IN A NUTSHELL® is a registered service mark of The Coronet Consulting Group.

to deliver what you really need to know, in as little of your valuable time as possible. This book is the direct result of that program.

The 12-Hour MBA Program proximately mirrors a "real" MBA course of study. It covers pretty much the same functional disciplines and objectives:

Marketing and Product Management	Develop new products and manage their growth.
Accounting	Understand key accounting principles and tax reduction methods.
Finance	Interpret financial statements and make savvy decisions.
Economics	Apply economic theory to everyday business situations.
Statistics	Grasp and use quantitative data to your full advantage.
Human Resources Management	Motivate your subordinates and peers, increasing productivity.
Operations Management	Use decision-making formulas for optimization of resources.
Technology Management	Learn sophisticated applications of old and new technologies.
Business Policy and Ethics	Gain the framework from which to formulate ethical decisions.
Strategic Planning	Establish objectives, strategies, and plans for the future.

As you can see, the major concepts and techniques taught in B-schools are taught here as well. Of course, you will learn the "textbook stuff" that you would otherwise be exposed to in an academic setting. However, you will not have to suffer through complicated formulas. They will be presented to you in a step-by-step manner that is very easy to understand. You will not even need to use a calculator. Just follow the instructions.

The 12-Hour MBA Program may not seem as thorough as the credential alternative. (For example, the inherent time constraint precludes the use of in-depth case studies.) It does, however, deliver three major benefits that few MBA programs offer:

1. The emphasis in this book is on practical and utilitarian applications rather than on the abstruse matter that a student may learn in order to pass an exam and soon forget, since it has little or no meaning in everyday business life. In configuring this program, I asked myself: "What are the 'special tips' and 'guerrilla tactics' that I would share with a younger brother or sister?" Such otherwise "off-the-record" advice is included in this book.

2. The chapter on education and career pathing (not an academic subject in the MBA curriculum) will serve as a guide to help you ascertain whether you really need the MBA degree or whether other degreed or nondegreed alternatives would be viable for your purposes.

3. There is a hidden "psychological agenda." Upon completion of reading *The 12-Hour MBA Program*, you will have a grounding in key concepts, techniques, and the terminology or jargon used by MBAs. Equally important, though, will be your sense of greatly increased confidence in your own new capabilities and enhanced ability to thrive in the business world, whether your goal is to function more effectively in an organizational environment and to climb the corporate ladder or to launch and operate a business enterprise of your own successfully. Since you will be operating on a level of competence and sophistication that is roughly equivalent in functional terms to that of MBAs, you certainly will have no cause to be intimidated by them.

Many MBAs would like you to believe that the study of business is extremely complex and difficult, almost surely beyond the comprehension of mere mortals. Although I very much appreciate all that I learned while studying for my MBA, I find this attitude arrogant, offensive, and totally unwarranted. In fact, some of the best and most successful business people I have come to know over the years lack higher education and an MBA. These executives . . . and millionaires . . . seem to have learned intuitively what others are taught in business school. And that can be boiled down to the following verities:

The successful operation of a business enterprise requires a *triple focus*, involving constant attentiveness to *the customer, the product, and the employee* (see Figure 1). After all, without the satisfied customer, there is no sale and, ultimately, no business. Similarly, we need the product (or service) to be of high quality or fair value to satisfy the customer's needs. And, of course, we need the employee who is well trained and properly motivated to facilitate delivery of the product in order to satisfy the customer's needs.

Toward this end, it can be said that the most sophisticated and prosperous organizations are those that are marketing driven, that is, dedicated to customer satisfaction; financially oriented, that is, geared

---

FIGURE 1   **TRIPLE FOCUS OF THE SUCCESSFUL BUSINESS ENTERPRISE**

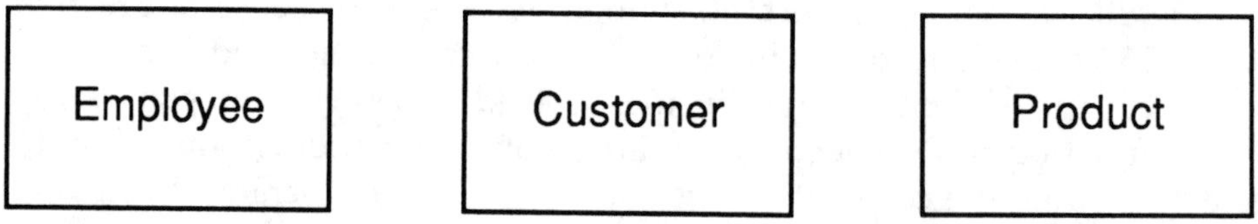

| Employee | Customer | Product |

toward positive cash flow, creative and flexible funding, and profitability; information and technology friendly, that is, embracing the state of
the art in information resources and technology, telecommunications and
other areas; and human resources sensitive, that is, hiring properly, developing and motivating employees (see Figure 2). Of course, the functional disciplines must be integrated. After all, marketing, finance,
information and technology management, and human resources management should not operate in a vacuum, independent of one another. They
must be strategically planned and managed, as well.

It is the aim of the MBA curriculum to develop the skills necessary
to plan and manage the various business disciplines. These different sets
of skills fall into three categories: "hard" skills, "soft" skills, and what I
shall refer to as "quali-quant" skills.

1. *"Hard" skills* involve quantitative or mathematical formulas. These
   enable us to succeed in a range of activities, including analyzing

**FIGURE 2   MULTIDISCIPLINARY AND
INTERDEPARTMENTAL APPROACH OF
THE SUCCESSFUL BUSINESS ENTERPRISE**

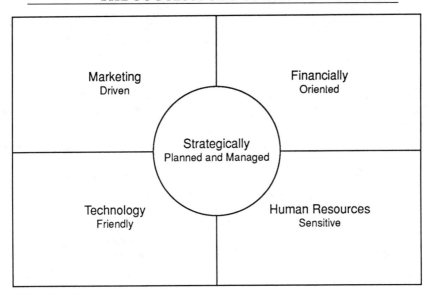

financial statements, improving cash flow, reducing tax liability, evaluating investment options, forecasting profits as well as the time horizons and completion dates of projects, utilizing material and human resources efficiently, pricing, and employing statistical data to arrive at the best possible decisions—and for political advantage.

2. *"Soft" skills* are qualitative or conceptual. These enable us to succeed in understanding and satisfying the customer in terms of developing the product, advertising and otherwise promoting the product efficiently, and (ultimately) facilitating its purchase. Drawing heavily upon the social sciences, "soft" skills also help us to succeed in understanding and satisfying the employee in terms of motivation, as well as management style and personality differences.

3. *"Quali-quant" skills* (sometimes referred to as Bayesian methods) are an amalgam of formulas and concepts designed to transform "soft" or subjective information (i.e., estimates) into a "harder," more objective, and, ostensibly, more reliable, form. Applications span the functional areas of the business environment.

The 12-Hour MBA Program has been instructionally designed so that the reader will be alternating between hard and soft skills throughout the program, with most of the quali-quant skills incorporated into Chapters 3 and 8.

Over the past six years, I have experimented with modifications in the curriculum and fine-tuned the program accordingly. To obtain the greatest possible benefit from this book, the following "ground rules" are strongly suggested:

1. Sit on a firm upright chair and use a desktop. Be sure there is adequate lighting. If possible, avoid telephone calls and similar interruptions.

2. Read the book in sequence and in its entirety. Do not skim or even glance ahead. The content is *gestalt* in nature. In other words, the whole is greater than the sum of its parts. (In fact, my students

often report a residual effect or delayed reaction to this learning experience, such that certain ideas become clear or "hit" them after completion of the curriculum.)

3. Take a 5- or 10-minute break on the hour. Research in the adult learning process indicates that many students suffer loss of concentration without brief rest periods. Try to complete at least one chapter per study session.

4. At the end of each chapter, reflect and ask yourself:

   a. How might I apply what I have just learned to my job or to my business?

   b. How might this relate to what I learned in the other chapters?

   c. What have I learned about how much I really know or don't know about the subject?

5. Be confident about your ability to turn the reading of this book into a rich learning experience. No previous business knowledge is required. The ability to read and to understand basic arithmetic functions will suffice.

6. Relax and enjoy.

CONTENTS

CHAPTER 1

MARKETING AND PRODUCT MANAGEMENT

Marketing involves those activities necessary for the planning and delivery of products (or services) from the producer (or performer) to the customer, to satisfy the customer and to meet the organization's objectives. These activities include:

- Product development
- Market research (including forecasting)
- Advertising
- Public relations (product publicity)
- Sales promotion
- Customer service
- Sales

DIFFERING SCHOOLS OF THOUGHT

Certainly, there may be ideological differences between departments within an organization, and often between members of the same

1

department as well. In fact, some individuals may claim to subscribe to a particular school of thought without truly understanding the implications of their positions. As this pertains to the marketing function, there are basically four ideological "camps":

The Product Concept

Ralph Waldo Emerson wrote, "Build a better mousetrap and the world will beat a path to your door." This concept—the *product concept*— suggests that the integrity of the product supersedes all other considerations and that quality alone determines the fate of the product. Therefore, no substantive marketing effort is required. A critical flaw in this approach is that potential customers may not even be aware of the product's existence, much less be able to evaluate it for purchase.

Another shortcoming is that "quality" may be subjective, differing from one individual to the next. (Surely, you've heard the saying, "One man's wine is another man's poison.") Those who subscribe to the product concept are often of the "techie" persuasion, with a background (or responsibility) in engineering, production, and operations management or a similar area.

The Selling Concept

The *selling concept* is predicated upon the notion that consumers will not make purchases in the absence of strong selling and promotional efforts. The negative stereotype of the automobile salesperson comes to mind in this regard. This individual has little concern for the consumer's well-being once the sale has been made. As a result, purchasers tend not to return. Surprisingly (or perhaps not), this doesn't bother the salesperson, since there are "a lot of fish in the sea." A major limitation of this position is that it greatly underestimates the cost of losing a customer and wrongly assumes that there is a rather infinite universe of potential customers from which to draw.

"Shirt-sleeves" salespeople with little exposure to other influences within the marketing function may be prone to this mind-set.

The financial people within their organizations, those who set or at least influence the setting of sales quotas, may also embrace the selling concept, in that they may, intentionally or otherwise, directly or indirectly, be pressuring the sales force to generate short-term profits at the expense of longer-term customer satisfaction.

The Marketing Concept

The *marketing concept* reflects the so-called "classical training" that MBAs receive. It is the premise that the company must conduct research to learn what the customer wants. Having done so, the *marketing mix* or 4 P's—*product, price, place* (channels of distribution), and *promotion*—are adjusted so that the customer will buy the product and use it with a high level of satisfaction. This approach complements the product concept, communicating the attributes of "the better mousetrap," and rather than assume that "the world will automatically beat a path to your door," makes that path to the company's door as attractive and easy to reach as possible. The marketing concept also tends to emphasize relationship-building, since (as we will learn later on) a company's future and long-term profitability ultimately depend upon satisfying the customer, not only initially, but repeatedly over time.

Marketing-oriented organizations such as Proctor & Gamble liberally employ "800" toll-free telephone numbers to address any concerns that customers might have. This is not as altruistic as it might seem. After all, the information that the company receives from the resulting telephone calls is, essentially, valuable and free market research.

If, for example, a sizable number of customers were to call and complain that they had found the corners of the Ivory soap bars they had purchased to be chipped, the company's product management team would almost certainly remedy the problem, perhaps by repackaging the product for greater protection. Moreover, P&G also unconditionally guarantees its products and offers refunds or exchanges, generally at the customer's option.

The Societal Marketing Concept

The *societal marketing concept* is actually a version of the marketing concept that includes the long-term welfare of the consumer and that of the general public as well. A notable success story in this category includes biodegradable laundry detergents in an age of ecological consciousness. However, the motorcycle manufacturing company that created a vehicle which reduced the loud, high-rpm sound typically associated with motorcycles to a quiet purr did very poorly with the product and was forced to abandon it. Apparently, the company's research and planning effort did not reveal what most of us probably suspect to be the cause: motorcycle enthusiasts actually *want* that noise.

In an organizational environment, policy decisions are often made by committee. The parties bring their various orientations to the table with them, so that even an organization which, on the whole, embraces the marketing concept may have "pockets" of countervailing forces. Therefore, the various influences we have just discussed rarely exist in pure form within the organization. (One might seriously question the desirability of an organization in which everybody shared the same influences and agreed on everything.)

CUSTOMER SERVICE AND CUSTOMER FOCUS

In marketing warfare, it is the customer service effort that supports the sales function, before and after the fact. This includes providing information to prospective and existing customers, resolving (or, better yet, avoiding) grievances, passively taking orders, and even (as in the more sophisticated marketing-oriented organizations) actively making sales. These activities are performed by the "foot soldiers" or "troops" who implement the policies established by "the brass," the organization's senior management. The nature of any customer service effort is determined to a large extent by the degree to which the organization's senior management truly values the customer. We refer to this orientation as *customer focus*.

Several Common Customer-Focus Issues

Does management dictate that the telephones be answered, "Thank you for calling XYZ Company. How may I serve you?" or is it okay merely to say, "XYZ Company"? It costs nothing to be courteous if not actually gracious and sets the tone for the conversation to follow.

Should the telephones be answered promptly (by no later than the third ring) even if this would incur additional cost, or is it okay to let the phones ring longer on the (totally incorrect) grounds that "If they want what we have, they'll wait"? Customers may wait this time if circumstances are pressing, but you can bet they'll take their business elsewhere in the future when they are no longer desperate.

If the customer is unhappy with a product and claims that it is defective, does the organization put the onus on the customer to make his case before a refund or credit is granted or does it immediately apologize for any inconvenience that may have been suffered and then immediately please the customer? Nordstrom, one of the most successful retail chains, is well known for its customer-focused approach. As one of the Nordstrom executives put it, "I don't care if they roll a Goodyear tire into the store. If they say they paid $200, give them the $200 (refund.)"[1]

Is Nordstrom out of its mind?

Not at all.

First, research reveals that the vast majority of people are basically decent and honest. One study involved sending researchers to pose as foreigners at airports, to hail taxicabs, and to see whether the drivers would earn their fares honestly or take the supposedly ignorant and hapless "foreigners" in circles for a much-inflated fare. It was found that only 2 of the 39 rides involved dishonest "joy rides." In fact, one driver actually warned his passenger to beware of people who would try to take advantage. So, if approximately 5 percent of all customers are dishonest and try to get away with something, Nordstrom might decide to build a 5 percent increment or "cushion" into its selling price and absorb its anticipated losses in order to avoid alienating an otherwise good customer. (By the way, it is not uncommon, with the passage of time, for customers to forget where they purchased items. To inform an ostensibly decent and honest customer that he or she purchased an item elsewhere, however tactfully it may be communicated, runs the risk of causing him or her embarrassment such that the individual might find it difficult to return as a patron.)

Secondly, research reveals that it costs approximately five times more to gain a new customer than to keep and continue to serve an existing customer. Think about it for a moment. Consider what it costs in time and financial investment. This includes, but is certainly not limited to, sales calls, written correspondence, telephone calls, advertising and promotion, travel and entertainment, and . . . I think you get the idea.

Idiosyncratic Credit

The concept of *idiosyncratic credit* comes from the domain of educational sociology. Researchers have observed that a schoolteacher is generally able to get his or her students to comply with what might be regarded as unreasonable requests or instructions, so long as these students perceived that the teacher is genuinely committed to their well-being.[2]

Abstracting this notion to the realm of commerce, I suggest that customers will be willing to bear with a panoply of your shortcomings (or those of your products), so long as they perceive that you (personally) and your organization (collectively) are genuinely committed to their well-being. One way to accumulate idiosyncratic credit is to list your home telephone number on your business card, to be called after-hours in the event of an emergency or crisis. You might initially be thinking: "No way will I let my business life intrude on my family or private life!" But consider the following:

The odds of a client having the legitimate need to call you after-hours is very small. If the need is any greater, then perhaps you need to improve your product or your performance and should welcome the call as an opportunity for product development or your continued on-the-job training. And, as corny or idealistic as it may sound, shouldn't you genuinely *want* to receive your clients' calls if they are actually in need? Consider, if you will, that their patronage pays for the food on your table. Moreover, they are people who have relied upon your claims and, just maybe, people whom you have come to know and like . . . and care about. And, if you really care about them, building idiosyncratic credit really isn't so . . . idiosyncratic . . . after all.

Consider this *impressive* "idiosyncratic credit" story:

During an emergency, H. Ross Perot, when he was chairman of Electronic Data Systems, took all his available vice presidents away from their desks and flew them, at great cost, to a warehouse located in a remote part of

Texas in order to count *by hand* the inventory levels of a small client whose computer-generated inventory reports would not otherwise be available on time. Now, if you were that client and you knew that the company you patronize was willing to go to such great lengths on your behalf, wouldn't you be inclined to remain loyal to that company and perhaps even expand your business relationship?

Consider this *cute* "idiosyncratic credit" story:

A shoemaker was asked to fix a pair of shoes that, as it turned out, were beyond repair. He returned the pair to the customer with a chocolate chip cookie wrapped in waxed paper inside each shoe, along with a note that said: *"Anything not worth doing is worth not doing well."*[3]

THE MACROENVIRONMENT

Marketers are affected by *exogenous variables,* those beyond our control. These include social, cultural, political, legal, technological, scientific, economic, and competitive factors. Although marketers may not be able to prevent certain events or scenarios from taking place, they are nonetheless potentially able to anticipate such occurrences and make contingency plans to address these changes. The key point here is to be proactive rather than reactive, to be an initiator rather than a victim of circumstances otherwise beyond your control.

For example, assume that you are the marketer of ready-to-eat packaged food products. Your research indicates that the percentage of the population consisting of well-paid, unmarried, urban professionals is large and increasing at a rapid pace. What might you do? Perhaps it would be a good idea to introduce a higher-priced line of single-portion gourmet meals.

DIMENSIONS OF BUYER PERCEPTION

The reasons that people decide to make a purchase or decline to do so can be boiled down to two primary dimensions and seven secondary dimensions that are corollaries of the primary ones. As you consider these (see

Figure 1.1), you may wish to assign a value, let's say from 1 to 10, for each of the dimensions relating to the product or service that you offer as an entrepreneur or manager. In a similar vein, you may wish to do much the same as it would pertain to your competitors' products or services. If you sell something business to business (e.g., from wholesaler to retailer or from raw materials to processing into another type of product), you may additionally wish to do this on behalf of your customers, to better understand their needs, latent or overt. In these ways, you may reach valuable insights about your offerings and perhaps become better able to identify strengths and weaknesses which you can then act upon.

Primary Dimensions

PERCEIVED RISK   Potential customers ask themselves, "How can this product harm me?" The greater the marketer's success in diminishing this perception of risk, the greater the likelihood of the purchase.

RELATIVE ADVANTAGE   Potential customers also ask, "How is this product better for me than my other alternatives?" The greater the marketer's success in increasing the perception of relative advantage associated with our product, the greater the likelihood of the purchase.

Secondary Dimensions

OBSERVABILITY   "Can the product's benefits be seen?" The more observable the benefits, the less the perceived risk and the greater the relative advantage. This might help to explain why it is often more difficult to sell services (which are not tangible) than it is to sell products (which are tangible). Astute marketers *add value* (or the perception of it) by including easy-to-use owner's manuals and by remaining in close touch with their customers, calling to their attention positive benchmarks or milestones. For example, an automobile dealer might call customers on the annual anniversary of a purchase to congratulate them and (not coincidentally) to inform or remind them that one year has passed without the need for any more than routine maintenance.

IMMEDIACY   "How soon will I see these benefits?" The more immediate the benefits, the less the perceived risk and the greater the relative advantage. (See the discussion of postpurchase dissonance later in this chapter.)

FIGURE 1.1 DIMENSIONS OF BUYER PERCEPTION

Perceived Risk

How will this product harm me ?

Relative Advantage

How is this product better for me than others ?

Primary
Dimensions

Observability

Can the products benefits be seen ?

Immediacy

How soon will I see these benefits ?

Complexity

Is the product easy to understand ?

Compatibility

Is the products usage congruent with attitudes,
opinions and belief systems ?

Secondary
Dimensions

Trialability

Will I be able to get a full refund or exchange if I
am not happy with the product ?

Availability

Will the product and related
accessories/services be available to me ?

Divisibility

Can I buy the product in a smaller quantity or
size or otherwise limit my purchase?

COMPLEXITY "Is the product difficult to understand and use?" The more complex the product is perceived to be, the less the relative advantage and the greater the perceived risk.

COMPATIBILITY "Is usage of the product congruent with my attitudes, opinions, and belief systems?" The more compatible the product is with my belief system, the less the perceived risk and the greater the relative advantage.

In the early days of mass marketing food products following World War II, the manufacturers of Duncan Hines cake mixes found that housewives were reluctant to buy their product despite the fact that the product's flavor, price, and other features were appealing. Ultimately, research indicated that housewives felt guilty about "making" a tasty cake that required very little effort. Given the gender stereotypes of the day, they believed that they should be working hard in their homes, since their husbands worked hard in their role as "breadwinners." So, what did the Duncan Hines folks do to overcome the resistance? They reconfigured the products so that the housewives would have to add an egg to the batter or recipe mixture, a nominal yet important symbolic effort . . . and the rest is history. Both Duncan Hines and the housewives (and their hungry families) were able to have their cake and eat it too.

TRIALABILITY "Can I use the product without making a permanent commitment?" The greater the opportunity to try the product, the less the perceived risk and the greater the relative advantage. Options can include refunds and exchanges, and in the case of lease arrangements, upgrades. Ultimately, customer-focused marketers must assume risks relating to trialability. If the product has merit and delivers on its claims, the issue is merely academic. If, however, customers are displeased with the product and choose to exercise their right of redress, marketers should view this as a cost, albeit potentially substantial, of doing business.

DIVISIBILITY "Can I buy the product in a smaller quantity or size or otherwise limit my purchase?" The smaller the quantity the customer can buy at one time, the less the perceived risk and the greater the relative advantage.

While this is not physically possible for certain types of transactions (i.e., one can't buy one-half of a car), minimum quantity requirements can be waived so that initial orders can be regarded, in effect, as "samples" for which the customer pays.

AVAILABILITY   "Are the product and its related accessories or services available to me?" The more available the product, the less the perceived risk and the greater the relative advantage. Increasingly, the focus is shifting from the "core" product to accessories, on the part of the consumer as well as the marketer. For example, anyone who has bought video game hardware (e.g., Nintendo) will probably have ended up spending more for the software accessories (e.g., additional programs for games) than they originally spent for the primary video game product.

For this reason, manufacturers of razor blades will make the hand razor apparatus (i.e., the item with a handle that holds the sharp blade in place) available to the consumer at low cost or perhaps even free of charge.

PARTICIPANTS IN THE BUYING PROCESS

While a single individual may be the one to authorize a purchase formally and perhaps even write a check, those who influence the purchase decision are often not readily apparent to the marketer. In organizations, it is often the secretary who recommends that a particular brand of word processing software be purchased, although the marketer may wrongly assume that it is this individual's boss who unilaterally makes the decision. Similarly, automobile dealers trying to make a sale to a married couple may, based upon sexist assumptions, take the liberty of focusing on the male spouse as the decision maker. Even if the wife were to have said something like, "Oh, Bob makes all the technical decisions about cars. Men know more about that kind of stuff," she may subtly—or not so subtly—be exerting her influence on "Bob's decision." She may, for example, lean toward an auto or brand that is more or less stylish, expensive, status oriented, practical, safer, comfortable, and so on. The dealer who does not identify and acknowledge her as an influencer, and perhaps as the ultimate decision maker, is likely to fail.

The definitive textbook case on this subject, the *gatekeeper effect*, involved observing mother and child shopping for breakfast cereal in supermarkets. The child was told by the mother to "choose" a cereal that he or she liked and wanted. But when the child actually "chose" a particular brand, the typical mother "vetoed" the choice (perhaps because the product contained too much sugar) and invited the child to make another choice or other choices until she approved.[4] Who, then, truly made these decisions? Needless to say, marketers of children's breakfast cereals typically seek Mom's approval.

THE RATIONAL BUYER VIS-À-VIS THE EMOTIONAL BUYER

Conventional wisdom has it that people who buy for their organizations are driven by a set of motives different from those of individuals who buy as consumers for their own personal needs.

The former has generally been regarded as *rational,* focusing on such objective considerations as price, quality specifications, promptness of delivery, and reliability; the latter, on the other hand, has generally been regarded as *emotional,* focusing instead on such subjective considerations as pride, guilt, sociability, and sensory satisfaction. Astute marketers understand that the dichotomy is not that clear and simple, that buyers for organizations respond to emotional appeals and that consumers in the general public respond to rational appeals, as well. This would help to explain the increased acceptance of such approaches as unit pricing (i.e., rational) for the general public of consumers (i.e., emotional) and celebrity endorsements (i.e., emotional) for business-to-business marketing (i.e., rational).

COGNITIVE DISSONANCE

Cognitive dissonance is the condition in which an individual is faced with conflicting emotions, attitudes, and actions. For example, an individual may know that cigarette smoking causes cancer but will smoke anyway.[5] Obviously, marketers should be concerned about any aspects of their products which bring cognitive dissonance to the fore. They should strive to minimize it as much as possible. Let us say that we are the marketers of a delicious dessert product. It is high in fat and cholesterol, both of which, we are told by authoritative sources, contribute to heart disease and other maladies. We might overcome these health concerns on the basis of any number of rationales, including moderation ("Everything is okay in moderation"), reward ("You worked hard and you deserve it" or, in a similar yet more familiar vein, "You deserve a break today"), and unbridled hedonism and inevitable mortality ("You only live once").

Note: The author is not in any way suggesting that marketers abandon their ethical responsibilities to consumers, promoting the use of a product that would ultimately harm them. (In the face of immediate threat, the product should be withdrawn from the marketplace, without equivocation. When the threat is less immediate or indirect, accurate representation and full disclosure are absolutely required.)

POSTPURCHASE DISSONANCE (ALSO KNOWN AS BUYER'S REMORSE)

Studies dealing with high-ticket purchases, in general, and automobile purchases, in particular, often characterize the buyer as second-guessing or regretting his or her purchase decision. (This might be triggered by a casual comment from a friend or relative such as, "Oh, your choice of Brand X is okay, but I've heard that Brand Y is a better value because . . . .") Marketers should anticipate this and can minimize or perhaps totally avert the problem by establishing an "800" toll-free telephone number to address questions and comments (particularly appropriate for technically oriented products, including computers and assemble-it-yourself items).

This is certainly not in lieu of having the salesperson and/or customer service representative follow up the transaction with telephone calls (the first one within one week and the others three to four weeks apart for the first couple of months), to thank the individual for his or her order and to make sure that the individual is totally satisfied with the product. If for any reason the customer is less than totally satisfied, the salesperson or customer service representative will have the timely opportunity to remedy the situation. Moreover, the salesperson may seize this moment as an excellent opportunity to sell the satisfied customer an upgrade on the original purchase or accessories or to obtain referrals among the individual's family, friends, and business associates.

DIMENSIONS OF MARKET SEGMENTATION

We live in a society in which individuality or individualism is tolerated, if not actually celebrated. That notwithstanding, even the most extreme of nonconformists ironically share certain characteristics with each other. When marketers are able to identify characteristics that people share and there is a substantial enough number of such people in this group that would seem likely to want to purchase their products, it can be said that the marketers would ostensibly target these groups—or segments. We call these processes *market segmentation* and *target marketing*, respectively. The most widely accepted and used criteria or dimensions for market segmentation include the following:

Demographic—those based upon such factors as age, gender, sexual preference, race, ethnicity, education, marital status, number of children or other dependents, income, and so on.

Geographic—those based upon such factors as neighborhood (typically identified by zip code), city, state, region, and so on.

Psychographic—those based upon attitudes, interests, and opinions (AIO). These may be sociocultural, religious/spiritual, philosophical, aesthetic, ethical/moral, political, economic, technological/scientific, curricular or extracurricular/occupational or personal, and so on.

Usage Related—those based upon how the product is actually used. *Quantity* is one such element. Marketers of beer know that their strategies and tactics must be different for appealing to heavy users (e.g., the stereotype of construction workers) rather than moderate users (e.g., the stereotype of "yuppies"). *Timing* is another element. Operators of movie theaters know that customers who attend on weekday afternoons may be a different breed from those who attend on weekend evenings, and they must adapt their strategies and tactics to address this. And, of course, the *application* or specific purpose of usage is critical. Purveyors of baking soda know that, while most customers use their product to prepare baked food items, these same individuals and other individuals may use the product as an odor absorbent (in refrigerators and in open spaces), a toothpaste, a poultice (for burns), a stain remover, and so on.

MARKETING STRATEGIES

Having identified market segments, marketers must then choose from *strategies* which best suit their objectives and limitations, as follows:

Concentrated Marketing—involves introducing a single version of a product that is designed to appeal to a single, particular market segment. This approach is well suited to organizations which have limited financial resources and/or enjoy an expertise specific to a particular type of customer base. Weight Watchers is an organization that employs this strategy, for the latter reason. It concentrates on serving those who are overweight or weight conscious.

Differentiated Marketing—involves introducing a number of different versions of a product, each designed to appeal to a different market segment. Generally, this strategy is adopted by organizations with substantial financial resources. They may have started out using a concentrated or undifferentiated marketing strategy and, as success and growth ensued, elected to develop a concentrated marketing strategy for two or more market segments.

General Motors and Ford Motor Company are organizations that employ this strategy. They both sell cars designed to appeal to many different types of consumers and/or to satisfy many different needs in the form of economy cars, sports cars, luxury cars, station wagons, vans, trucks, and so on.

Undifferentiated Marketing—involves introducing only a single version of the product in the hope that it will appeal to an entire universe of consumers, an appeal to the lowest common denominator. Once upon a time, when life was simpler, when the world wasn't quite so fragmented and market segments didn't exist or perhaps, more accurately, were not readily identifiable or even thought of as significant, this approach was the norm. Prior to the days of Classic Coke, Diet Coke, Caffeine-free Diet Coke, Cherry Coke, and the myriad other versions of Coke, there was plain old Coke or Coca-Cola. And, in contrast to the previous example for the differentiated marketing strategy, Ford Motor Company limited its original product offering, the Model T, not only to a single version but to a single color. ("You can have any color you like, so long as it's black.")

PRODUCT POSITIONING

Using the technique of *product mapping* to graphically depict market segments relative to product attributes, we may endeavor to "match" market segments to (competing) product options. (To be precise, we should actually be referring to "brands" or competing versions within a product class.) In Figure 1.2, we have divided our universe of potential customers into quadrants, established by a vertical HI-LO axis for price and another

FIGURE 1.2   PRODUCT POSITIONING

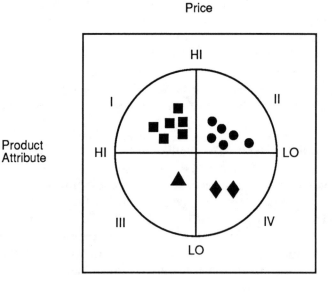

horizontal HI-LO axis for a particular product attribute. In this instance, the attribute relates to the degree to which the product is high or low in fat and calories. Quadrant I is characterized by a brand high in fat and cholesterol and in price as well. The square icons are indicative of the potential number of customers in this quadrant or market segment. Assuming that each of these icons represents many potential customers and that they are configured in a cluster formation, this would indicate that there very well may be a market for high-priced and rich (i.e., high-in-fat) food products. Similarly, the circles in quadrant II indicate that there may also be a market for high-priced diet (i.e., low-in-fat) food products. However, the triangles and diamonds in quadrants III and IV, respectively, suggest that the markets for low-priced rich food products as well as low-priced diet food products may be not be sufficient to justify the investment and marketing effort.

MARKETING RESEARCH

How do marketers obtain such information and other information necessary to make informed decisions? (See "Conducting A Research Project" in Chapter 4 on Statistics.)

THE MARKETING MIX

Whatever it is that you are marketing, it has four dimensions. These *4 P's* are *product, price, place* (i.e., channels of distribution), and *promotion.*

Product

A product is an item or service that is offered to the consumer, to satisfy his or her needs and to realize organizational goals.

Product Differentiation

Aside from customer focus, no concept is more important for marketers than that of product differentiation, that is, the effort to distinguish favorably one's brand from all other brands within its product class. Some brands are intrinsically differentiated. For example, a brand of ice cream which has a higher butterfat content than any of its competitors is, objectively speaking, a richer offering than those of the competition. Yet other brands are extrinsically differentiated or perceived as distinguished from the competition based upon their brand images rather than substantive elements. For example, there is a popular brand of beer whose TV commercials depict famous athletes telling jokes and otherwise enjoying each other's company. The fellow watching this commercial is not going to buy this beer because of its purportedly superior flavor, but will buy it, consciously or otherwise, because he would enjoy the company of these athletes and would like to join them. By buying and consuming the brand, he vicariously joins them.

What are the tools available to marketers to differentiate their brands and to protect their valuable interests?

TRADEMARKS AND SERVICE MARKS   These legal claims are designed to protect the goodwill that your brand name, corporate name, slogan, or logo succeeded in establishing. Trademarks are granted for an initial period of 10 years, but can be renewed. Consider, if you will, how terrible it would be for McDonald's if other hamburger marketers could get away with calling their offerings Big Macs. In some instances, a trade name is so powerful that it is virtually synonymous, in the mind of consumers, with the name of the product class in which it competes. In referring to those little sticks with cotton on the end that we use for personal hygiene and cleaning in crevices, many of us (and I'm guilty of this) ask for Q-Tips® rather than *cotton swab sticks*. If I were about to sneeze, I might ask if someone could spare a Kleenex® rather than facial tissues.

The strongest form for protection of claim is that of the *registered trademark* (for products or tangibles) or *registered service mark* (for services or intangibles). This is typically denoted by the symbol ® or the words, "Registered Trademark." It is required that the applicant formally file a claim with the Patent and Trademark Office. Once this has been done, a reasonable period is allowed to transpire in which any parties who wish to challenge the claim may do so. If no such challenges are made or if these are ruled to be lacking in merit, then the claim is granted. Trademarks can be renewed indefinitely every ten years.[6] (However, a trademark may be considered abandoned if it is not used for two years once the claim has been made.)

Another option is the *common law trademark* or *service mark*. Marketers may affix "TM" (for products) or "SM" (for services) under common law without formally filing a federal claim. (This is roughly analogous to the manner in which an unbetrothed couple who have cohabited for years and have borne children together may be regarded, under common law, to be married in the eyes of the law.) It is recommended that "TM" or "SM" be used until application for a federally registered mark is finally approved. While neither affords the degree of protection that the registered trademark affords, and may necessitate a greater burden of proof if the mark is challenged, each does provide public notice of claim. Also, each can be used immediately, whereas the registered mark can only be used after the claim has been approved. (Prior usage is in violation of federal law and may subject the offender to penalties.)

COPYRIGHTS These legal claims are designed to protect intellectual properties against unauthorized usage. These must be presented in fixed form rather than just as "ideas" and may include but are not necessarily limited to fiction and nonfiction texts, musical compositions, works of art, dramatic works, photographs, and computer software programs. *Ownership of copyright* exists when the work is completed in any fixed form regardless of date of registration with the Copyright Office. However, the ability to defend a challenge to one's claim would certainly be enhanced by formally filing claim with the Copyright Office. The duration of copyright in the United States initiated in or after 1978 is 50 years after death of the author. However, each country has its own applicable copyright laws, such that duration of the copyright may extend to as much as 70 years after the author's death.

Notice is generally characterized by the word "Copyright" or the symbol © followed by the year in which the work was actually completed in fixed form and the copyright owner's name. If the work is presented in audio format (e.g., phonograph, audiocassette, compact disc), notice for the work in fixed form for this type of medium is generally characterized by the symbol ℗ followed by the year in which the work was produced in that medium and the copyright owner's name. If the entity is, say, an audio version (i.e., recorded spoken word performance) of a book or collection of poems, it would be appropriate to include two copyright notices: one for the intellectual property (© for the book or collection of poems) and the other for the audio version (℗ for the spoken word performance).[7] (In fact, the very book you are now reading is protected by copyright law.)

In some instances, lack of copyright can have catastrophic consequences. The computer software developer who creates an absolutely brilliant program but neglects to copyright the work may find that his work is being misappropriated (read: ripped off) and that he may have no remedy after a certain period of time, after which the work becomes public domain. As a matter of policy, marketers should place copyright notices on virtually *all* marketing communications materials such as brochures, proposals, audiovisual presentations, advertisements, sales promotion items, and more. It costs nothing and establishes a claim for exclusive use of the properties in fixed form, discouraging competitors from bearing the fruits of your labors. (By the way, the greater importance of copyright is further underscored and gravely dramatized by the contention that Adolf Hitler might never have been able to commence hostilities against England were it not for his control of the copyright on his book, *Mein Kampf.* By restricting publication in England and other soon-to-be-allied-nations to the original German language version, he was able to distort public opinion in those countries by concealing his evil intentions and delaying earlier and timely mobilization against his armed forces.)[8]

PATENTS   *Patents* are legal claims designed to protect a mechanical or scientific process, instrument, method, or design. Common law patents do not exist as such. The single meaningful option is formally filing a claim with the Patent and Trademark Office. Patents are characterized by display of the "Patent # XXXX" notice once the period for challenges is over and the claim has been granted. Until the patent is granted, the "Patent Pending" notice is affixed.

Patents are granted for a nonrenewable period of 17 years. They then expire, and other parties cannot be prevented from using them.

The sound quality of your favorite music recordings may have been enhanced by means of the Dolby® noise reduction system, a patented method. Your apparel will not shrink by more than a minute percentage when you launder it if it was Sanforized® or treated with the once-patented Sanforization process. An almost endless list of products is currently or previously has been protected by patents, from dynamite to the zipper, the electric guitar to the refrigerator. Recently, ethical controversy has erupted over legal rulings enabling entrepreneurs to patent gene splicing techniques. Critics contend that patent protection should not extend into the domain of genetic engineering.

Product Life Cycle

Just like human beings, *products have a life cycle,* too. They are *conceived* (i.e., via research and development), *born* (i.e., launched), *grow, mature, decline,* and eventually, *die.* There are particular characteristics of each stage and corresponding marketing implications. Astute marketers manage the product life cycle to greatest advantage, elongating the product's life cycle and/or its generation of cash (see Figure 1.3).

FIGURE 1.3 PRODUCT LIFE CYCLE

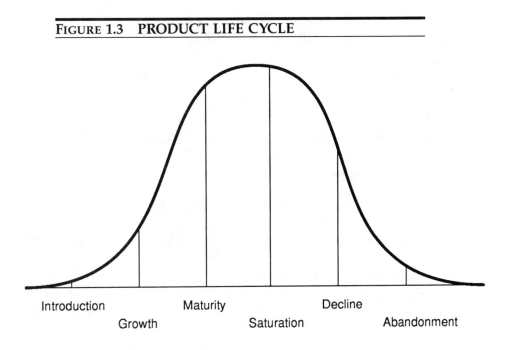

Introduction   Maturity   Decline

Growth   Saturation   Abandonment

INTRODUCTION   This stage is characterized by research and development. Sales and profits are usually very low, although costs may be substantial. This underscores the importance of adequately budgeting for or funding the project. (This point is worthy of greater discussion and will be addressed in Chapter 2.)

GROWTH   This stage is characterized by increased sales and profits. Heavy promotional costs are often incurred.

MATURITY   This stage is characterized by "peaking" and attempted maintenance of sales levels. It is possible to increase sales, but this would almost surely incur substantial costs. Profits may already have begun to diminish, and this may be related to a very high level of competition.

SATURATION   This stage is characterized by decreased profitability linked to costs. Competition increases even more so. The goal, at this juncture, is to maintain market share. However, this is often not possible.

DECLINE   This stage is characterized by perceived futility in the attempt to maintain market share. Typically, this is accompanied by cost cutting.

ABANDONMENT   At this stage the product's performance no longer merits inclusion in the organization's product line.

The Boston Consulting Group Growth Share Matrix

In conjunction with the product life cycle, the *BCG model* provides a valuable framework that enables us to identify and evaluate our products relative to market share and the extent to which the market, as a whole, is expanding or contracting (as shown in Figure 1.4).

Products may be categorized as follows:[9]

- *Star*—product with high market share in a high-growth market, every mother's prayer.

- *Problem Child*—product with low market share in a high-growth market; mother is concerned because her child is not growing as anticipated. Another perspective is that mother shouldn't be quite so concerned if the child has carved out a little niche that is impervious to the competition; maybe slow yet consistent growth isn't so bad.

FIGURE 1.4   THE BOSTON CONSULTING GROUP GROWTH-SHARE MATRIX

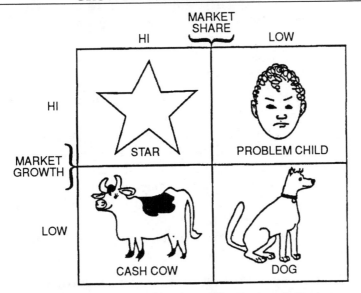

*The Experience Curve: The Growth-Share Matrix or the Product Portfolio (Boston Consulting Group, 1973).

- *Cash Cow*—product with high market share in a low-growth market. Since the cow is generating milk (i.e., cash), the marketer may elect to "milk the cow dry," so to speak, accelerating cash flow and, not coincidentally, the product life cycle.

- *Dog*—product with low market share in a low-growth market. In this sense, "dog" is certainly not "man's best friend." Rather, it is analogous to "bomb" (i.e., something that fails miserably) or to "lemon" (i.e., something that is defective or undesirable). So it would seem that we would want to drop the dog from our product line.

PRODUCT LINE INCLUSION OR EXCLUSION   However, there may be circumstances under which doing so may ultimately have deleterious consequences for the entire product line, for example, the dog just happens to be the "flagship" brand or that which people readily identify with the company's product line. (Do you remember the uproar that ensued when Coca-Cola withdrew the original or "old" Coke from the marketplace, replacing it with the "new" Coke?) Another instance in which abandonment may be damaging might relate to the company's identity or image as a "full-service" resource. By dropping the product from its line, the company can no longer accurately claim to be a full-service entity. What, then, are some of the practical options?

BUNDLING   We may choose to package or bundle the product with other offerings in our product line. Cable TV system operators commonly use this approach, offering, say, five pay TV channels for the price of four, in the hope that cable viewers will subscribe to more channels than they otherwise would if they were able to buy "à la carte" (i.e., each channel separately). By doing so, both parties may be perceived to have succeeded. The entrepreneurs gain by increasing their absolute sales volume. Moreover, they increase profitability by taking advantage of the economies of scale they enjoy from purchasing their programming in larger quantities. (See Chapter 3 for greater elaboration on this point.)

RAISING THE PRICE   By increasing the selling price sufficiently, we may be able to keep the product in our line, since the profit margin may be acceptable even though sales volume in absolute dollars may leave something to be desired. This option would allow the entrepreneur to maintain the image of being a full-service entity without having to lose money on the product offering.

Price

Price, one of the 4 P's of the marketing mix, is what the customer pays for the product or service. Pricing options include the following:

Premium Pricing

Also known as "skimming the cream," this option involves charging a high price relative to other brands within the product class. This can be an effective approach if it succeeds in, or at least lends support to, creating the perception of high quality. In other words, a product can be differentiated on the basis of price. (In my personal experience as an educator and consultant, I have found that consumers are generally far more reluctant to pay a price that is perceived as "too low" than one that is "too expensive.") The product category of cosmetics is one in which brand image (i.e., extrinsic differentiation) rather than objective and substantive product attributes tends to determine how well a product will fare. The contention is supported by the fact that cosmetics has one of the highest advertising-to-sales ratios of any industry or product class.

Let's discuss Clinique, a respected marketer of high-end cosmetics. One of its products, an astringent, consists almost entirely of alcohol. If we were to pay a visit to our local drug store, we would find that a similar bottle of alcohol would cost perhaps only 10 percent of what we would pay for Clinique astringent. Even if Clinique were to add other chemicals or substances to its astringent, the percentage of the product's cost that this would represent would be very small indeed and, I suggest, might not objectively justify a price that is so high.

So, how does Clinique, which I view as an excellent product line of high quality, justify its price? For one thing, it appears to position itself as a "medically approved" product, and this is in no way contradicted by the company's policy of dressing the sales representatives who staff their retail counters in white laboratory-type coats.

Fair Pricing

This option involves charging a price that is objectively regarded as reasonable based upon market research. Ivory soap and Miller beer are examples of brands successfully employing this approach.

Penetration Pricing

This option involves charging a low price on the assumption of selling the brand in enormous quantities. This is based upon a strategy of profit through volume. McDonald's does it with burgers, and Bic does it with disposable pens, lighters, and razors.

Parity Pricing

This option involves setting a price that roughly matches those of competing brands within the product class. This approach may suggest that the marketer is not attuned to the importance of differentiation.

Cost-Plus Pricing

This option involves setting a price that factors in a given profit margin (e.g., cost plus 25 percent). This approach may indicate a preoccupation with investment return and can be particularly unfortunate in the absence of a proper customer focus orientation. The marketer may be oblivious to price sensitivity in the marketplace and competitors' pricing tactics.

Keep in mind that whatever option is chosen, it must be congruent or consistent with the other components of the marketing mix. If, for example, the product is of extremely high quality and of an "exclusive" nature, a high or premium price would seem to be appropriate.

Place

Place, another of the 4 P's of the marketing mix, is that component that deals with the product's channels of distribution or how it is conveyed from the producer to the end user. Its functions include manufacturing, transportation, warehousing, wholesaling, and retailing. The more of these functions that the company is willing to assume, the greater the percentage of selling price it can command. If an organization controls all the channels of distribution for its product, we say that it is vertically integrated. The manufacturer acquiring a company in order to have access to the raw materials it wishes to use in its own products is integrating backward (i.e., toward the source of supply or seller), whereas the wholesaler acquiring retail outlets to expand distribution is integrating forward (i.e., toward the source of demand or buyer).

There are essentially three distribution options, as follows:

- *Intensive*—aims for maximum exposure. The product is sold through any responsible wholesaler or retailer who will stock it. This pertains especially to convenience goods and so-called impulse or point-of-purchase items, such as razor blades or candy.
- *Elective*—aims for moderate exposure. The product is sold through "better" retailers. This pertains especially to shopping goods or "high-ticket" items, such as home entertainment centers or appliances.

- *Selective*—aims for limited exposure. The product is sold by a single dealer within each trading region. This pertains to specialty goods, those which are highly differentiated or luxury items.

Promotion

Promotion involves communication of product attributes and corporate image in the most favorable light possible (without misrepresentation) to intermediary sellers (i.e., trade advertising and trade promotion) and to end users (i.e., consumer advertising and consumer promotion). Sophisticated mass-marketing organizations (Procter & Gamble immediately comes to mind) typically employ a "pulling" strategy in regard to promotion (see Figure 1.5). By heavily promoting their products directly to the consumer via advertising and sales promotion, the company hopes to create a strong demand which is then felt by the retailer who is

FIGURE 1.5   THE "PULLING" PROMOTIONAL
                       STRATEGY

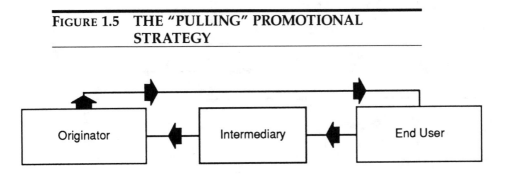

virtually "forced" by requests from customers to order and stock the product. The retailer, in turn, pressures the wholesaler to order and stock the product, and so on. Thus, if the manufacturer has succeeded, it can be said that the product has been "pulled" through the channels of distribution by strong demand. This approach is in sharp contrast to a "pushing" strategy (see Figure 1.6), in which demand is stimulated from manufacturer to wholesaler to retailer to end user, essentially "pushing" the product through the channels of distribution. (The "pulling" strategy does not, however, preclude a strong direct selling effort. It would only tend to lessen the resistance of potential customers, since much of the influence leading to a sale will have been accomplished by advertising and promotional efforts.)

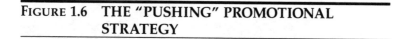

FIGURE 1.6   THE "PUSHING" PROMOTIONAL
STRATEGY

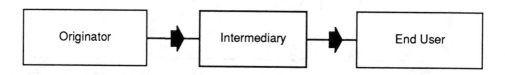

Dimensions of Advertising Effectiveness

There are a number of key elements we must consider in creating effective advertising:

DEMOGRAPHIC   What type(s) of people do we want to influence?

GEOGRAPHIC   Where are the people we want to influence?

IMPACT   Is the desired message well communicated and hard hitting enough to be memorable? To spur purchase? Generally, advertising is designed to address the "AIR" concerns:

- Does it make the consumer *aware* of the product?
- Does it *inform* the consumer about the product's attributes?
- Does it *remind* the consumer about that which is already known?

Basic rules of thumb are:

1. The "KISS" approach—"Keep It Simple, Stupid!"
2. The 3 T's—"Tell 'em what you're going to tell 'em."
   "Tell 'em."
   "Tell 'em what you've told 'em."

REACH   How many individuals or households will experience one exposure of the message?

FREQUENCY   How many times will these people experience the message?

DURATION   How long is the message?

TIMING   When will the message be experienced?

COST (per thousand; also known as CPM)   How much does it cost to reach 1,000 people or households with a single exposure? The formula for calculating CPM, the primary measure of relative efficiencies between media options, is as follows:[10]

$$CPM = \frac{\text{Media cost}}{\text{(Audience measured in thousands)}}$$

For example,

	Advertising Media		
	A	B	C
Cost of ad	$10,000	$30,000	$10,000
Audience	100,000	600,000	500,000

so CPM is as follows:

$$\text{A: } \frac{\$10,000}{100,000} = \$100$$

$$\text{B: } \frac{\$30,000}{600,000} = \$50$$

$$\text{C: } \frac{\$10,000}{500,000} = \$20$$

So, as we consider placing an ad with media options A, B, or C, we find (using the CPM formula) that C offers a more favorable CPM than does A or B ($20 as compared to $100 or $50, respectively). (However, the option with the best CPM does not necessarily offer as large an audience as competing options. In this particular case, C offers five times the audience of A at the same cost and five-sixths of B's audience at one-third the cost.

Media Options

What are the major advantages and disadvantages of the various media we may elect to use?

BROADCAST TV

- High reach (potentially many millions of people).
- High impact (audio and video, stereo, and color. Animation is particularly important for demonstrating how a product is used.).
- High cost (in relative and absolute terms).
- Low selectivity regarding demographics (anyone with a TV can tune in, whether a millionaire or welfare recipient).

CABLE TV

- Moderate to high reach.
- High impact.
- Moderate to high cost.
- High selectivity regarding demographics (cable channels can segment on the basis of special interests, such as sports, music, etc.).

RADIO

- Low to high reach.
- Limited impact (audio only; but stereo is good for music programming). Listeners may experience the medium passively, while working, reading, or as "background." Nonetheless, they may become active buyers who, if driving home during rush hour, may pull off the road to purchase an impulse food item just advertised on the program they are listening to.
- Low to moderate cost.
- High selectivity regarding demographics (radio programming segments on the basis of such formats as music type, talk show, etc.).
- Lead time is generally very short. In fact, commercials can even be read "live" on the air, offering as much immediacy as any medium can be expected to.

MAGAZINES

- Low to high reach.
- Moderate to high impact. (Multicolor printing on glossy paper is well suited to upscale or aesthetically oriented items.)
- Moderate to high cost.
- Very high selectivity regarding demographics.
- Lead times of up to three months from submission of art and copy to hitting the newsstands is a major disadvantage, since timely response to market conditions might not be possible.

NEWSPAPERS

- Low to high reach.
- Moderate to high impact.
- Moderate cost.
- Moderate selectivity.

Unlike magazines, lead times are generally very short, sometimes only a couple of days or less.

DIRECT MAIL

- Low to high reach, depending almost entirely upon the degree to which the marketer is willing to invest in the purchase of mailing lists, postage, and other variable costs.
- Low to moderate impact.
- High cost per person reached.
- Extremely high selectivity (can cross-reference mailing lists to identify ideal prospects).

INTERNET   (See "Internet" in Chapter 6 on Technology Management.)

- High reach (worldwide access).
- High impact (audio and video, stereo and color, as well as animation are ideal for product demonstration).
- Extremely low cost. Although designing and maintaining a web site may cost thousands of dollars, CPM can be extremely low.
- At first glance, rather low selectivity regarding demographics. After all, virtually anyone with a computer, modem and connecting software can explore the Internet. However, with the adroit use of "search engines," web publicity releases and sophisticated "click here" options within the web site, selectivity can actually be very high.

OUT-OF-HOME MEDIA   This category includes miscellaneous media, such as "Goodyear-type" blimps, billboards, and more. Can you believe

that there is a company that leases the bottoms of the 18 holes of golf courses, so that golfers (who are often corporate decision makers) will bend down to pick up their golf balls out of the holes only to be greeted by a message like, "Reach out and touch someone."

- Low to high reach.
- Low to moderate impact.
- Low cost.
- Low to moderate selectivity.

Sales Promotion Tools and Activities

Sales promotion has long been the "black sheep" in the promotion mix, and undeservedly so. It has been observed that sales promotion expenditures tend to increase as advertising expenditures decrease, and vice versa. The following represent key sales promotion areas of involvement:

PREMIUMS   *Gift with Purchase (GWP)* involves giving an additional item for free as an incentive to buy a product (e.g., "Buy this, get that free). *Purchase with Purchase (PWP)* involves selling an additional item as an incentive to buy a product (e.g., "Buy this, get that at a highly discounted price"). Initially, both GWP and PWP were regarded as innovations in the marketing of cosmetics. Due to their early success, however, they have become industry standards. Research indicates that consumers will often switch from one brand of cosmetics to another if the brand they have been buying fails to offer premiums as appealing as those of competitive brands.

DISCOUNTS   Simply put, a discount is a reduction in price (see Elasticity of Demand in Chapter 5).

"TWOFERS"   Offering two units for the price of one constitutes a "twofer." In effect, this is a type of discount.

COUPONS   Coupons are documents, often in the form of clippings from print media or as stand-alone promotional pieces, which entitle the bearer or presenter to discounted or free merchandise or service.

SAMPLES   Giving away the product for trial at no charge is a sample strategy. This is perhaps among the very best ways to demonstrate a product's superiority. Sampling puts all on the line, suggesting that the consumer try the product and judge for himself or herself. This may be a particularly appropriate tactic for attracting consumers to a new brand, especially if the marketer is up against competing brands backed by heavy promotional expenditures. The potential and substantial downside, obviously, is that the brand's claim of superiority must be backed up in its product attributes. Therefore, extensive pretesting would seem to be in order.

CONTESTS   Contests generally award prizes to winners of a competition that may involve coming up with the slogan for a product, solving a puzzle, and so on.

SWEEPSTAKES   Sweepstakes award prizes based upon a random drawing. Unlike contests, sweepstakes do not require skill, specialized knowledge, or creative input.

INCENTIVES   In trade promotion (i.e., business-to-business), incentives are rewards based upon specific or targeted performance. For example, a manufacturing company may, for a specific and limited period of time, award a cash "bonus" or "spiff" to each salesperson of the retail establishments it supplies for each unit of the manufacturer's product that the individual sells. Another option is to offer a prize, be it a cash award or something of value such as a vacation, to the salesperson in each retail location who sells the most of this manufacturer's product (or a specific brand).

PRODUCT PUBLICITY   Product publicity actively brings the product to the attention of the public and/or specialized constituencies via media exposure and special events. Issuance of press releases and related marketing communications are involved. Opportunities may include:

- *Articles and/or interviews* in the broadcast and print media
- *"Staged" events* (i.e., "the world's largest . . . .")
- *Trade/professional association lectures and demonstrations*
- *"800" toll-free telephone numbers* to provide information
- *"Audio- or video-cassette programs* to provide information

- *"Freebie"* (i.e., free or complimentary) *distribution* of the product accompanied by information to "opinion leaders," whose opinions are well regarded and can generate positive *"word of mouth."*

Sales

There are many entities that espouse a particular "method" for selling. Ultimately, all of these may be viewed relative to two models, the consultative model and the AIDA model. Neither model must be adopted in its entirety. One can "cherry pick" the best aspects of each to come up with his or her own particular approach to best address such considerations as personal style, customer preferences, cultural and industry norms, as well as time urgency.

THE CONSULTATIVE MODEL   This approach is based upon keen listening skills, identification of the potential customer's real and perceived problems, and the sales professional's ability to find a solution to these problems. The major strength lies in its customer-focused orientation, whereas its major weakness is that the sales pro tends to assume a more passive and nondirective role. In addition, time constraints (not to mention a lack of candor) may limit the opportunity for the customer to share his or her problems.

THE AIDA MODEL   This approach is based primarily upon the power of persuasion and identification of the potential customer's real and perceived problems. AIDA's primary strength is that it allows the sales professional to play an active and somewhat directive role in the process. The model's primary weakness is that it may be regarded as coercive and, therefore, not sufficiently customer focused.

The sale is accomplished in stages that must follow in sequence.

1. *"A" for Attention.* You must have the customer's attention. Otherwise, there is no point in proceeding.

2. *"I" for Interest.* Sample gambit: "Sir, my research department and I have studied your organization and, based upon our preliminary findings, we can reduce your xxxx costs by $300,000 per month." (Continue, explaining in detail.)

3. *"D" for Desire.* Sample gambit: "Ms. Johnson, as you can see, using our service will save your organization a lot of money. As a further inducement . . . and given that we will come to agreement today, I will include an additional month of service at no extra charge."

4. *"A" for Action.* After having answered any questions that the potential customer might have, the next and most important step is to close the sale or ask for the order, taking action. (And, by the way, many a sale is lost simply *because the salesperson does not know how to ask for the order* or even *completely fails to make the request.*)

   Sample gambit: "I'm glad that you can see the tremendous value of our service. Since we seem to be in agreement on all that's been discussed, I'd very much appreciate your approval." ("Approval" is a euphemism of sorts for "signature." Keep in mind that we live in a litigious society and that putting one's name on paper may have a chilling effect.)

5. Once the deal is done, leave or adjourn the meeting as soon as possible. Since you have accomplished your goal, there is nothing to gain by lingering. In fact, it can only go downhill if you do.

CROSS SELLING

This is a key concept for sales professionals. Since time is money and the opportunity to meet with potential or existing customers may be limited as well, it becomes all the more important to turn a single sales transaction into another or into multiples during the same sales meeting or as a direct result of it (not to mention the enhanced economies of scale that can be enjoyed; see the economies of scale discussion in Chapter 5).

Figuratively speaking, if customers are willing to buy peanut butter from you, they might also buy jelly from you. And if they do, they may also be interested in buying some bread from you. Now, if you are particularly skilled and the latent need is identifiable and sufficiently strong, you might even succeed in selling some fresh, cold milk . . . to wash it all down, of course! Caveat: Don't make the cross-sales unless the customer is very pleased with the primary or core product that introduced you to the cross-selling opportunity in the first place. Why? Because, as sophisticated and ethical marketers, we engage in relationship-based selling.

RELATIONSHIP-BASED SELLING

We must constantly look at the big picture and our commitment to *serve the customer well over the long term.* If need be, we must be willing to walk away from the sale we know we can close, if this would endanger our more enduring relationship with the customer; no hit-and-run approach here. This may be justified in terms of the marketing concept, idiosyncratic credit, and the true cost of losing a customer.

THE MARKETING AND PRODUCT MANAGEMENT CHECKLIST

1. How can I accumulate more idiosyncratic credit with my customers?

2. Have I adequately appraised the macroenvironment and been proactive in planning?

3. What can I do to minimize the sense of risk and maximize the sense of relative advantage that potential or existing customers may perceive regarding purchase of the products I sell?

4. Who actually makes the decision to purchase my products and who else participates in the decision?

5. Am I targeting the most appropriate market segments?

6. What can I do to differentiate my brands further from others competing against it in the same product class?

7. Are the 4 P's of my marketing mix congruent with each other, and does the mix work to the greatest advantage?

8. Do my advertising, promotional, and selling strategies best communicate the products' attributes and my commitment to customer satisfaction?

RECOMMENDED READING

Kotler, Philip, *Marketing* (Englewood Cliffs, NJ: Prentice Hall, 1987).

Levitt, Theodore, *The Marketing Imagination* (New York: Collier
Macmillan, 1983).

Rachman, David J., *Modern Marketing* (New York: Dryden Press,
1980).

Stanton, William J., *Fundamentals of Marketing* (New York: McGraw-
Hill, 1991).

ORGANIZATIONS AND RESOURCES

American Association of Advertising Agencies
666 Third Avenue
New York, New York 10017
(212) 682-2500

American Marketing Association
250 S. Wacker Drive, Suite 200
Chicago, IL 60606
(312) 648-0536

Marketing Education Association
1908 Association Drive
Reston, VA 22091
(703) 476-4299

National Foundation of Sales Executives
Statler Office Tower, Suite 458
Cleveland, OH 44115
(216) 771-6650

ENDNOTES

1. Nancy Yoshihara, "Chain Sets Itself Apart with an Old-Fashioned Service Policy," *Los Angeles Times,* September 30, 1984, part V, pp. 1, 17.

2. David H. Hargreaves, *Interpersonal Relations and Education* (London: Routledge & Kegan Paul, 1972).

3. Robert Fulghum, *All I Really Needed to Know I Learned in Kindergarten* (New York: Villard Books, 1988).

4. L. Berey and R. Pollay, "The Influencing Role of the Child in Family Decision Making," *Journal of Marketing Research,* Vol. 5, February, 1968, pp. 70–72.

5. Leon Festinger, *A Theory of Cognitive Dissonance* (Evanston, IL: Row Peterson, 1957).

6. U.S. Trademark Association, *U.S. Trademark Source* (New York: U.S. Trademark Association, 1992).

7. M. William Krasilovsky, Esq., personal communication, February 1993.

8. Robert B. Downs, *Books That Changed the World* (New York: New American Library, 1983), p. 317.

9. David A. Aaker, *Developing Business Strategies* (New York: John Wiley and Sons, 1984).

10. David A. Aker, *Pocket Guide to Media Terms and Media Math* (New York: Media Resources and Research, J. Walter Thompson USA, Spring 1984).

CHAPTER 2

ACCOUNTING
AND FINANCE

Finance deals with analysis of past and present data for the purpose of deploying or investing the organization's monetary and capital resources to greatest advantage. It combines day-to-day cash management responsibilities with long-term planning objectives. The function of accounting provides us with a valuable framework for management decision making toward this end, and we refer to this specialty within the discipline as *managerial accounting*. The specialty that deals with such matters as compliance with governmental regulations (such as tax and securities laws), documentation for operational purposes (i.e., recordkeeping or bookkeeping) as well as internal control for the safeguarding of the organization's assets is known as *financial accounting*. Our discussion of accounting will focus almost exclusively upon the managerial. And since the underlying premise here is decision making, we will cover accounting and finance in the same chapter, referring back and forth to integrate the two disciplines and for ease of understanding.

FINANCIAL STATEMENTS

The keystone source of financial information is an organization's *annual report*. (Publicly held organizations are required by law to file these, whereas privately held entities are not required to do so.) This document includes the *balance sheet, income statement,* and *cash flow statement.* These financial statements must be prepared in accordance with *generally accepted accounting principles (GAAP),* the body of universal standards for the accounting profession, specifically *certified public accountants (CPAs).* In addition, auditors must certify that the information contained in the statements is presented fairly, in accordance with *generally accepted auditing standards (GAAS),* the body of universal standards specific to auditors or accountants who prepare financial statements for the annual report.

In the annual report, we find a section entitled *Management's Discussion and Analysis (MD&A).* This is an important preliminary and subtle indicator of management's assessment of problems and opportunities as well as its plans for the future. While it would be unrealistic to expect management to acknowledge fault in the wake of its poor decisions and their consequences, it would be at least as troubling to investors in the enterprise if management were to rationalize the problems and/or fail to chart a credible and achievable course for the future to remedy these.

Notes to Financial Statements are "footnote" explanations to the information provided in the financial statements, but can actually be as important as the statements themselves. These notes may disclose significant developments such as outstanding lawsuits, changes in accounting methods or officers' compensation structure, and reorganization or sales/purchases of business units.

Balance Sheet

The balance sheet represents a "snapshot" of a business at a particular point in time (see Figure 2.1). It reveals what the company owns (assets), what it owes (liabilities), and its net worth (shareholder's equity). The balance sheet doesn't "wipe clean" to zero at the beginning of each new period (i.e., December 31 to January 1). Assets are listed in order of

FIGURE 2.1 BALANCE SHEET

Your Company, Inc.
(as of December 31, 1992; in millions)

Assets

Current assets

Cash	$ 15.5
Marketable securities	3.0
Accounts and notes receivable	4.0
Inventories	16.5
Total current assets	$ 39.0

Property, plant, and equipment

Buildings, machines, and equipment	190.0
Less: Accumulated depreciation	−19.5
Land	5.5
Total property, plant, and equipment	$176.0

Other assets

Receivables due after 1 year	8.5
Other	1.5
Total assets	$225.0

Liabilities and Shareholders' Equity

Current liabilities

Accounts payable	$ 25.0
Accrued liabilities	6.5
Current maturity of long-term debt	2.0
Federal income and other taxes	12.5
Dividends payable	1.0
Total current liabilities	$ 47.0

Other liabilities	6.0
Long-term debt	27.0
Total liabilities	$ 80.0

Shareholders' equity

Preferred stock	15.0
Common stock	45.0
Additional paid-in capital	20.0
Retained earnings	65.0
Total shareholders' equity	$145.0
Total liabilities and shareholders' equity	$225.0

liquidity, while liabilities are listed in order of claim. The synopsis of the formal "formula" for the balance sheet is:

$$\text{Assets} = \text{Liabilities} + \text{Shareholders' Equity}$$

I believe that you will find it more meaningful, however, to move "Liabilities" to the other side of the "equal" sign, so that the informal "formula" reads:

$$\text{Shareholders' Equity} = \text{Assets} - \text{Liabilities}$$

Income Statement

The income statement represents the profitability of a business over a period of time. Unlike the balance sheet, it does "wipe clean" at the beginning of each new period. The origin of the income statement has been traced back to the ancient days of Cassius, who rented slaves and used a crude form of this financial statement to record his revenues (e.g., rental fees) and expenses (e.g., fig leaves used to cover the slaves' private parts). The "informal" synopsis of the "formula" is:

$$\text{Gross income} - \text{total expenses} = \text{Net profit (loss)}$$

This formula is derived as follows:

(1) Operating income (loss) = Sales − total costs and expenses

Total costs and expenses are composed of:

Cost of goods sold

Sales, general, and administrative expenses

Depreciation

(2) Income before taxes = Operating income − interest charges

(3) Net income (loss)   = Income before taxes − provision for taxes

Net income (or net loss) represents the net profitability of the organization. This is commonly referred to as its *bottom line*. And it is important to keep in mind that it is what you get to keep that really counts (net income) rather than what you earn (operating income).

Referring to the income statement in Figure 2.2, let us explore and try to reach some preliminary conclusions about Your Company, Inc. In comparing figures for 1991 and 1992, we find the following:

Sales

Sales increased from $90 million to $100 million, up about 11 percent. Not bad. However, consider the following:

Cost of Goods Sold

Cost of goods sold increased from $50 million to $59 million, up about 18 percent. This hike outstrips the rate of inflation and, perhaps

FIGURE 2.2   INCOME STATEMENT

Your Company, Inc.
(year ended Dec. 31; in millions)

	1992	1991
Sales	$100.0	$90.0
Cost of goods sold	59.0	50.0
Sales, general, and admin. expenses	15.0	20.0
Depreciation	12.0	10.0
Total costs and expenses	$ 86.0	$80.0
Operating income	$ 14.0	$10.0
Interest charges	0.5	1.0
Income before taxes	$ 13.5	$ 9.0
Provision for income taxes	5.0	4.0
Net income (loss)	$ 8.5	$ 5.0

more important, is in excess of the percentage increase of sales. Perhaps we should ponder the following:

- Can we reduce the cost of goods sold by renegotiating our deals with suppliers or by finding new and less expensive suppliers?
- Can we reduce the cost of goods sold by purchasing in larger quantities and, if so, would this be efficient?
- Can we substitute different substances, materials, or products for the ones we are currently buying?
- Can we raise the price of our product?

Sales, General, and Administrative Expenses

This category decreased from $20 million to $15 million, down about 25 percent. As a general rule, when expenditures decline dramatically (as is this case), it can be assumed that this is the result of deliberate management action. (Conversely, substantial growth in expenditures may be the result of "creeping decimalism," wherein management is not sufficiently sensitive to the notion that increments in spending, however small, ultimately can add up to a large sum.) We might ask:

- Does the decrease reflect a diminution in labor? In other words, were people fired or was the company "downsized" (to use the corporate euphemism)? If so, what were the direct and indirect costs associated with severance, outplacement, and replacement?
- Does the decrease reflect a reduction in salaries or commissions payable to the organization's salespeople or independent sales agents?
- Does the decrease reflect a tightening of the purse strings regarding employee expense accounts or employee benefits?
- Does the decrease reflect reductions in such areas as office rental, utilities (e.g., telephone, electric), and insurance? If so, what are the trade-offs?
- Does the decrease reflect a cutback in research and development? If so, how is this likely to affect future earnings?

Total Costs and Expenses

This category increased from $80 million to $86 million, up about 7.5 percent. We might question:

- How does this rate compare with that of inflation?
- How does it compare with standards for the industry?
- Can this category of expenditures be pared down further without adverse effects?

Depreciation

Depreciation increased from $10 million to $12 million, up about 20 percent. Given that depreciation is indicative of the potential for tax reduction arising from wear and tear or obsolescence of equipment or property (more on this later in the chapter), we might ponder:

- Does the increase reflect additional purchases of equipment or property, or does it reflect a change in the method of depreciation that is used?

Operating Income Vis-à-Vis Net Income

Operating income (i.e., income before interest charges and taxes) increased from $10 million to $14 million, up about 40 percent, a substantial rise. Yet net income (i.e., income after interest charges and taxes) increased at an even greater rate, 70 percent. Does this suggest that management was able to reduce its indebtedness and/or take greater advantage of tax reduction opportunities in the second year? Or was it a stroke of luck that interest rates (and, therefore, interest expense) went down? It is noteworthy that, in absolute dollars, interest charges are relatively low and were reduced by about 50 percent. And, although provision for income taxes is substantial relative to income before taxes (which increased by about 50 percent), it increased at a rate of about 20 percent, rather less than the rates of increase for operating income, income before taxes, and net income.

Cash Flow Statement

This statement depicts sources and uses of cash over a given period of time. Focus is on generating income and honoring obligations (e.g., loans and other debts). It is of the utmost importance to differentiate the concepts of profitability and cash flow. An organization's balance sheet may reveal assets that substantially outweigh liabilities (i.e., profitability). However, if these assets are not collectible (e.g., bad debts or accounts receivable in arrears) or liquid (e.g., inventory) within a given time frame, then it is more than just theoretically possible that the

---

FIGURE 2.3   CASH FLOW STATEMENT

Your Company, Inc.
(year ended Dec. 31; in millions)

	1992
Cash flows	
Sources: Operating Activities	
Net earnings	$ 8.5
Accounts and notes receivable	(2.5)
Inventories	(5.0)
Depreciation	12.0
Accounts and notes payable	0.0
Federal income and other taxes	(1.0)
	$ 12.0
Sources: Investing Activities	
Marketable securities	.5
Property, plant, and equipment	(16.0)
	$(15.5)
Sources: Financing Activities	
Preferred stock (sale)	3.0
Common stock (sale)	2.5
	$ 5.5
Cash, net change	$ 2.0
Cash, on January 1	$ 13.5
Cash, on December 31	$ 15.5

organization might be unable to meet its obligations and be forced to file for bankruptcy even though financial statements indicate "profitability." As the saying goes, "Positive cash flow, not profit (on the books), pays for lunch."

Cash flows fall into any of three categories: *operating activities, investing activities,* and *financing activities.*

Referring to the cash flow statement in Figure 2.3, let us continue to explore and try to reach additional preliminary conclusions about Your Company, Inc. Given that figures in parentheses indicate money that is spent whereas figures without parentheses indicate money that is received, we observe that operating activities yielded $12 million, positive cash flow thus far. However, investing activities indicate that $15.5 million was spent in excess of that which was received. What might have precipitated this? The expenditure of $16 million for property, plant, and equipment suggests that the organization is implementing a plan for expansion. This possibility is supported by the sale of $5.5 million in preferred and common stock under financing activities. Why sell stock to raise capital rather than take a bank loan? Perhaps the organization wanted to avoid paying interest on the principal, or (as we will see in the upcoming section on Key Financial ratios) maybe it couldn't qualify for a loan. Ultimately, the organization posted a net positive cash flow of $2 million. In other words, although some activities may have contributed to positive cash flow while others may not have, the result is that more money was received than was spent.

TAX REDUCTION CONSIDERATIONS

Referring to the income statement (Figure 2.2), it is clear that an organization's net income or "bottom line" can be enhanced by a reduction in tax obligations much as it is by increased revenues and operating income. Essentially, the organization typically accomplishes this on a number of different fronts.

Structure of the Organization

Assuming that the entity is a corporation (rather than a partnership or sole proprietorship), different categories of the corporation (e.g.,

"C" or "S") are taxed at different rates. It may even make sense to switch from one type to another as tax status changes. In addition, the state (or province) in which the corporation is chartered can similarly influence tax liability.

Timing of Purchases

Most accounting is done on what is known as the *accrual basis.* Using this method, revenues are recognized on transactions during the tax period in which they actually occur. Conversely, if revenues are recognized during the period in which payment is made, we can assume that accounting is done on what is known as the *cash basis* (see Figure 2.4). Deferring the transaction even a single day (from December 31 to January 1, based on a January 1 fiscal year) essentially causes revenues to be recognized in the more recent year. If income is high in a given year, the organization may benefit from being able to "write off" deductible expenditures against such income in the same year, effectively reducing its taxable income. If, however, income was very low or the organization has already written off a great deal for this year, it may elect to defer additional purchases until the following year when it can "use" the deductions.

Timing of Bad-Debt "Write-offs"

Accounts receivable which are substantially in arrears may, in fact, be uncollectible. Conceptually similar to the previous example of timing of purchases, the organization may elect to recognize such "write-offs" at a point in time when these deductions can be taken to full advantage. (It is interesting to note that Citicorp's write-off of $3 billion in Latin

FIGURE 2.4 REVENUE RECOGNITION

Method	When Revenue Is Recognized	Purchase (or) Payment December 31	January 1
Accrual	At time of purchase	X	
Cash	At time of payment		X

American debt in 1987 may have held strategic implications beyond those relating to the reduction of potential tax liability. Citicorp was at the time the largest U.S. bank, with assets far in excess of the vast majority of its competitors. Since market conditions dictated that these competitors would have to "follow the leader" and write off their own Latin American debt, Citicorp enjoyed a relative advantage. Its size allowed it to "take the hit" or bear the loss better than its competitors.)

Depreciation

The government allows the organization to reduce its tax liability by acknowledging the decrease in value of equipment and property relating to wear and tear or obsolescence. Depreciation policies can change to reflect the attempts of government to stimulate growth of particular industries or of the economy, in general.

There are three depreciation methods. Using a purchase of $80,000 in equipment and a life span of four years, for example, the methods are:

1. *Straight Line*—Simply divide the purchase price of the item by the number of years over which it is to be depreciated. So, when we divide $80,000 by 4, we find that $20,000 is the amount that we can depreciate for each of the four years.

$$\text{Year 1: } \$80,000 \times 1/4 = \$20,000$$
$$\text{Year 2: } \$80,000 \times 1/4 = \$20,000$$
$$\text{Year 3: } \$80,000 \times 1/4 = \$20,000$$
$$\text{Year 4: } \$80,000 \times 1/4 = \$20,000$$

2. *Double Declining Balance*—Take the straight line and double it. In the previous example, one-fourth of the depreciation takes place in each of the four years; in this instance, we depreciate at the rate of one-half of the (remaining) value for each year.

$$\text{Year 1: } \$80,000 \times 1/2 = \$40,000 \text{ (balance carried to year 2)}$$
$$\text{Year 2: } \$40,000 \times 1/2 = \$20,000 \text{ (balance carried to year 3)}$$
$$\text{Year 3: } \$20,000 \times 1/2 = \$10,000 \text{ (balance carried to year 4)}$$
$$\text{Year 4: } \$10,000 \times 1/2 = \$\,5,000 \text{ (balance is not exhausted)}$$

You will notice that the value has not been fully depreciated by the end of the fourth year, since the balance is repeatedly multiplied by a fraction and is, therefore, almost infinite. So, when you reach the year when the straight-line method offers greater depreciation than the double-declining balance method, you may elect to switch over to the straight-line method to exhaust the value in its entirety.

3. *Sum of the Years' Digits*—Sum the weighted value of the years $(4 + 3 + 2 + 1 = 10)$ and use this number as the denominator of the fraction for rate of depreciation, wherein each year serves as the numerator. (Note: This method is archaic and not commonly used.)

$$\text{Year 1: } \$80,000 \times {}^4/_{10} = \$32,000$$
$$\text{Year 2: } \$80,000 \times {}^3/_{10} = \$24,000$$
$$\text{Year 3: } \$80,000 \times {}^2/_{10} = \$16,000$$
$$\text{Year 4: } \$80,000 \times {}^1/_{10} = \$\ 8,000$$

As you can see, these methods differ in the rate at which depreciation is paced. Generally speaking, we would prefer to accelerate depreciation as much as possible to reduce income taxes.

Inventory Valuation: LIFO/FIFO

The means by which we assign value to our inventory also can have tax reduction implications. Since inventory falls into the category of assets and is reflected in the income statement under cost of goods sold, diminishing or enhancing inventory will affect the bottom line. Let's assume that we operate a furniture store and have a total of three identical chairs. One chair was purchased in February for $12, another in March for $14, and still another in April for $17. If we sell a single chair, we might ask whether this item was the one we bought in February for $12 or the one bought in April for $17. If we decide that the "February" chair (the item purchased earliest or first) is the one that we will sell first, then we are using the *FIFO method (first in, first out)*. If, on the other hand, we decide that the "April" chair (the item purchased most recently or last) is the one that we will sell first, then we are using the

---

FIGURE 2.5 IMPACT OF LIFO/FIFO ON VALUE OF INVENTORY

	Value of Inventory	
	FIFO	LIFO
1 chair bought in February for $12	(Sold)	$12
1 chair bought in March for $14	$14	$14
1 chair bought in April for $17	$17	(Sold)
	$31	$26

LIFO method (last in, first out). In this situation, the FIFO method enhances the value of the inventory, as shown in Figure 2.5, whereas the LIFO method diminishes it.

Since LIFO relatively understates the value of inventory, it may serve to reduce taxable income. However, management might prefer FIFO if, for example, a key priority is raising capital. In this case, the relatively overstated value of inventory may serve to enhance net worth in the balance sheet, due to the increase in the value of inventory, an asset. It may also serve to enhance net income, reflected in the income statement as a reduction in the cost of goods sold. And this might appeal to potential lenders and investors. (FIFO and LIFO assume that prices increase with time as a result of inflation.)

INTERNAL CONTROL

The organization must establish and implement policies and procedures to safeguard assets. The following measures are time honored and widely accepted:

- Make responsibilities as clear and discrete as possible. For example, only one salesclerk should be assigned to a given cash register per shift, and that individual should be held accountable for any shortage.

- Create a division of labor in areas where there is a potential for abuse. For example, don't allow an employee to control cash if he or she also functions as the bookkeeper or to control inventory if he or she is the shipping department manager.

- Set up a system of checks and balances. For example, require two signatures on checks, for access to lockboxes, and for authorization of electronic funds transfers (EFT).

- Hire reliable and ethical personnel. Toward that end, job interviewers should view the reference check as more than just a minor and routine procedure. Off the record, I suggest that interviewers pose the following "acid test" question near the end of the reference check protocol: "Would you rehire him/her if he/she were available?" Any hesitation or response short of unequivocal endorsement is a red flag.

- Document control procedures wherever and whenever possible. These measures are ideally immediate, complete, and tamper-proof. For example, cash register receipts must be given to each customer to document and ensure that each transaction is actually rung up by the clerk rather than pocketed by that individual. It is also a good idea to post a notice conspicuously at the cash register to let customers know that they are entitled to a store credit (of, say, $10) if the clerk fails to hand them a register receipt. This provides an incentive to the customer to report an unrecorded transaction.

- Rotate duties periodically. This enables management to observe whether or not a problem stops when an individual is temporarily removed. If it does stop, this suggests that the individual may be culpable. Vacations provide such an opportunity. (For this reason, bank officers are required to take a vacation of at least two consecutive weeks in duration.)

- Utilize independent checks. Hire outside specialists such as certified public accountants in the capacity of auditors to inspect for irregularities or flaws in the system.

- Supervise closely (as needed) and monitor performance (periodically, albeit regularly).

OTHER PEOPLE'S MONEY (OPM)

Savvy businesspeople understand the importance of this concept. In simplest form, OPM suggests that you arrange to receive money due to you (i.e., receivables) at the earliest possible moment, and arrange to send money that you are obligated to pay (i.e., payables) at the last possible moment. In this way, you are able to enjoy the *float* or interest earned on this money. OPM policies are associated with improved cash flow as well as profitability.

IMPROVING CASH FLOW

The following methods are time honored and widely used. While MBAs may learn these in classrooms, successful "shirtsleeves" managers often know these intuitively or learn them on the job:

Incoming Money (accounts receivable, money that is owed to you)

- Have payments electronically wired directly into your bank account via electronic funds transfer (EFT). This can be done almost instantaneously. If this is not possible or feasible, have payments mailed directly to the bank (i.e., lockbox) rather than to you. The day or two saved in this process allows your money to be earning interest that much longer.

- If your organization has many locations or branches, use the concentration method. Funds from all areas are instantaneously transferred to a main or central bank account. As a result, your organization will pay less in fees for bank services while collecting more interest.

- Allow cash discounts for early payment. You might, for example, grant a 2 percent discount for payment within 10 days (i.e., "2%, net 10 days"). Caveat: The author is reluctant to suggest this because even 2 percent net 10 days is the equivalent of more than 24 percent annualized. Moreover, creditors may pay you late and take the discount anyway.

- Bill customers on a timely basis. "Age" your accounts, tracking them to see if they are past due and, if so, 30-60-90 days past due or more. If sufficiently delinquent, immediate payment may be demanded and further credit denied. Billing should be on a cyclical basis (e.g., weekly). In this way, pressure on the accounts receivable function is eased and operations tend to run more smoothly.

- Make an active collection effort. This may involve progressive steps ranging from initial telephone calls and letters to sterner demands and warnings of legal action.

- Deposit receipts on a daily basis. In addition to the OPM factor, this makes good sense from the standpoint of internal control as well. (Cash, checks, and credit card forms can be lost or stolen.)

- Factor accounts, if necessary. Essentially, this involves selling your accounts receivable to a financial services company at somewhat less than face value. Of course, the factor then assumes full responsibility for collection.

Outgoing Money (accounts payable, money that you owe)

- Centralize accounts payable and pay at the last possible moment. (See discussion of OPM on previous page)

- Draw checks on out-of-town banks to take advantage of the "float," since it will take longer for the checks to clear.

BUDGETS

The budget represents the official position of management relative to anticipated financial activity within a given time frame (generally, quarterly and annually). It may be used to authorize action (i.e., spending as the budget allows), to assess performance (i.e., using the budget as a standard of measure), and to motivate (i.e., granting financial awards such as a bonus to those who surpass the budget standard).

There are, of course, different types of budgets to suit different purposes. *Operating budgets* govern everyday expenses, while *capital budgets* govern major investments and are more closely linked to strategic rather than operational planning (see Chapter 8 on strategic planning). Zero-based budgets require decision makers to start from scratch (i.e., zero dollars), assuming that previously accepted expenses are not automatically included in the upcoming budget. Each expense must be justified in its own right, regardless of how it was represented in previous budgets. (This method, associated with a cost-cutting or "bean counter" mind-set, is commonly employed within certain rigid organizational cultures and seems to become even more widely used during periods of economic downturn. While this approach can uncover areas of unnecessary spending, it more often than not generates excessive paperwork and is, ironically, more costly in the end.)

TIME VALUE OF MONEY (DISCOUNTED CASH FLOW)

Simply put, $1 today is worth more than $1 a year from now, due to inflation. Clearly, the value of money diminishes with the passage of time. With this in mind, we factor (or "discount") these future cash flows to reflect this diminution in value.

INVESTMENT APPRAISAL

Organizations must acknowledge the reality of *limited funding resources* (as reflected in budgets, for example) in the face of what may seem to be an abundance of investment opportunities. This area of endeavor is known as *capital rationing*. It implies that financial decision makers sometimes reach a fork in the road, so to speak, and must choose one investment or another, but not both. The potential benefit associated with the forgone option is known as an *opportunity cost*. Conversely, a chosen investment may, in time, come to be regarded as an undesirable and irrevocable action (as in the decision to buy equipment that has unforeseeably become obsolete and whose value will not be recouped). This potential burden is known as a *sunk cost*. There are basically three methods of assessing potential investment opportunities. Two of these, *net present value*

(NPV) and *internal rate of return (IRR),* address the issue of discounted cash flow. The *payback method* does not.

Net Present Value (NPV)

NPV weighs the investment in absolute dollars against its return in discounted cash. The formula for NPV is:

> NPV = Discounted incoming cash flows (revenues)
> − outgoing cash flow (investment) at the outset

Let us assume that we are presented with an investment opportunity which would cost us $3,800 in today's money. Let us further assume that we can reasonably expect to generate $1,000 in income per year for each of five years and that the prevailing cost of money or interest rate is 8 percent.

Do we accept or decline the opportunity?

The answer lies in comparison of the discounted (incoming) cash flows to the initial (outgoing) cash investment. We multiply each year's projected incoming cash flow by its discount factor (see shaded area under "8%" in the present value table, Figure 2.6). If the sum of the discounted cash flows is a higher figure than the amount invested, it would seem (other factors aside) that we should accept the deal. If the sum is lower, it would seem (other factors aside) that we should decline the deal. In the example at hand, we would accept, since the difference between the two, the NPV, is a positive figure, 193. In choosing between several investment options, we would generally select the one with the highest NPV (other factors aside).

Investment (outgoing cash flow)		$3,800
Revenues (incoming cash flows)	Year 1: $1,000 × 0.926 =	$ 926
	Year 2: $1,000 × 0.857 =	$ 857
	Year 3: $1,000 × 0.794 =	$ 794
	Year 4: $1,000 × 0.735 =	$ 735
	Year 5: $1,000 × 0.681 =	$ 681
	$5,000	$3,993
	(Not discounted)	(Discounted)

$3,993 (discounted income) − $3,800 (initial investment) = $193 (NPV)

FIGURE 2.6   PRESENT VALUE OF $1

Period

	1%	2%	3%	4%	5%	6%	7%	8%	9%	10%	12%	14%	15%
1	.990	.980	.971	.962	.952	.943	.935	.926	.917	.909	.893	.877	.870
2	.980	.961	.943	.925	.907	.890	.873	.857	.842	.826	.797	.769	.756
3	.971	.942	.915	.889	.864	.840	.816	.794	.772	.751	.712	.675	.658
4	.961	.924	.889	.855	.823	.792	.763	.735	.708	.683	.636	.592	.572
5	.951	.906	.863	.822	.784	.747	.713	.681	.650	.621	.567	.519	.497
6	.942	.888	.838	.790	.746	.705	.666	.630	.596	.364	.507	.456	.432
7	.933	.871	.813	.760	.711	.665	.623	.683	.547	.500	.452	.400	.376
8	.923	.853	.789	.731	.677	.627	.582	.540	.502	.467	.404	.351	.327
9	.914	.837	.766	.703	.645	.592	.544	.500	.460	.424	.361	.308	.284
10	.905	.820	.744	.676	.614	.558	.508	.463	.422	.386	.322	.270	.247
11	.896	.804	.722	.650	.585	.527	.475	.429	.388	.350	.287	.237	.215
12	.887	.788	.701	.625	.557	.497	.444	.397	.356	.319	.257	.208	.187
13	.879	.773	.681	.601	.530	.469	.415	.368	.326	.290	.229	.182	.163
14	.870	.758	.661	.577	.505	.442	.388	.340	.299	.263	.205	.160	.141
15	.861	.743	.642	.555	.481	.417	.362	.315	.275	.239	.183	.140	.123
16	.853	.728	.623	.534	.458	.394	.339	.292	.252	.218	.163	.123	.107
17	.844	.714	.605	.513	.436	.371	.317	.270	.231	.198	.146	.108	.093
18	.836	.700	.587	.494	.416	.350	.296	.250	.212	.180	.130	.095	.081
19	.828	.686	.570	.475	.396	.331	.276	.232	.194	.164	.116	.083	.070
20	.820	.673	.554	.456	.377	.312	.258	.215	.178	.149	.104	.073	.061
25	.780	.610	.478	.375	.295	.233	.184	.146	.116	.092	.059	.038	.030
30	.742	.552	.412	.308	.231	.174	.131	.099	.075	.057	.033	.020	.015

Period

	16%	18%	20%	24%	28%	30%	32%	40%	50%	60%	70%	80%	90%
1	.862	.847	.833	.806	.781	.758	.735	.714	.667	.625	.588	.556	.526
2	.743	.718	.694	.650	.610	.574	.541	.510	.444	.391	.346	.309	.277
3	.641	.609	.579	.524	.477	.435	.398	.364	.296	.244	.204	.171	.146
4	.552	.516	.482	.423	.373	.329	.292	.260	.198	.153	.120	.095	.077
5	.476	.437	.402	.341	.291	.250	.215	.186	.132	.095	.070	.053	.040
6	.410	.370	.335	.275	.227	.189	.158	.133	.088	.060	.041	.029	.021
7	.354	.314	.279	.222	.178	.143	.116	.095	.059	.037	.024	.016	.011
8	.305	.266	.233	.179	.139	.108	.085	.068	.039	.023	.014	.009	.006
9	.263	.226	.194	.144	.108	.082	.063	.048	.026	.015	.008	.005	.003
10	.227	.191	.162	.116	.085	.062	.046	.035	.017	.009	.005	.003	.002
11	.195	.162	.135	.094	.066	.047	.034	.025	.012	.006	.003	.002	.001
12	.168	.137	.112	.076	.052	.036	.025	.018	.008	.004	.002	.001	.001
13	.145	.116	.093	.061	.040	.027	.018	.013	.005	.002	.001	.001	.000
14	.125	.099	.078	.049	.032	.021	.014	.009	.003	.001	.001	.000	.000
15	.108	.084	.065	.040	.025	.016	.010	.006	.002	.001	.000	.000	.000
16	.093	.071	.054	.032	.019	.012	.007	.005	.002	.001	.000	.000	
17	.080	.080	.045	.026	.015	.009	.005	.003	.001	.000	.000		
18	.089	.051	.038	.021	.012	.007	.004	.002	.001	.000	.000		
19	.080	.043	.031	.017	.009	.005	.003	.002	.000	.000			
20	.051	.037	.026	.014	.007	.004	.002	.001	.000	.000			
25	.024	.016	.010	.005	.002	.001	.000	.000					
30	.012	.007	.004	.002	.001	.000	.000						

Note: If additional outgoing cash flows were to be incurred in subsequent years, they too should be discounted. In such an instance, the previous NPV formula would be modified as follows:

NPV = Discounted incoming cash flows (revenues)
      −outgoing cash flow (investment at the outset)
      − discounted outgoing cash flows (investment in subsequent years)

Internal Rate of Return (IRR)

Unlike NPV, IRR weighs the investment relative to the cost of money or interest rate, which herein is an unknown. IRR assumes that NPV is zero. In other words, IRR asks us to determine the rate of interest that would cause the discounted (incoming) cash flows to be equal to the investment (i.e., zero difference). Using the example for NPV, we would calculate to find the rate that would, in effect, reduce $3,993 to $3,800. That figure is your IRR and is calculated by trial and error. In this particular instance, that rate is slightly higher than 9 percent (see shaded area under 9% on the present value table, Figure 2.6). The investment would be judged desirable to the extent that the IRR exceeds those of alternative investment options.

Investment (outgoing cash flow)		$3,800
Revenues (incoming cash flows)	Year 1: $1,000 × 0.917 =	$ 917
	Year 2: $1,000 × 0.842 =	842
	Year 3: $1,000 × 0.772 =	772
	Year 4: $1,000 × 0.708 =	708
	Year 5: $1,000 × 0.650 =	650
	$5,000	$3,889
	(Not discounted)	(Discounted)

The amount—$3,889 (discounted income at 9 percent)—is still a little higher than $3,800 (initial investment). To reduce the discounted income by $89 and set it equal to the initial investment ($3,800 = $3,800, zero difference), we would require an IRR of slightly higher than 9 percent.

Payback

The payback method helps us to calculate the point in time at which we can expect to recoup our investment. Unlike net present value and internal rate of return, however, payback does not discount cash flows. (If the deal takes place within a short time frame, say, one year, then the time value of money would probably not be as significant a factor and, for this reason, payback is a commonly used "quickie" method.) Also, payback does not evaluate the upside or profitability of one investment option as compared with another. Let us compare Deal A, which yields income of $50,000 per year for 7 years, with Deal B, which yields $50,000 per year for 10 years (see Figure 2.7). Each deal requires an investment of $250,000. Using the payback method, we would rank these options equally, since each recoups its investment or reaches payback in 5 years (i.e., $50,000 per year for each of 5 years). However, Deal B generates $500,000 (i.e., $50,000 per year for each of 10 years), whereas Deal A generates only $350,000 (i.e., $50,000 per year for each of 7 years), a difference of $150,000 without discounting of cash flows.

Special Considerations Regarding Foreign Investment

In addition to using the appraisal methods we have just discussed, it is necessary to weigh certain factors specific to foreign investment and operations. For example, *fluctuations in currency exchange rates* can render an otherwise profitable situation unprofitable. *Unfavorable tax structure* can have a similar effect. In addition, some countries place *restrictions on outbound transfer of funds,* making it difficult or impossible to withdraw capital for reinvestment or redeployment. And, of course, *political instability* may portend nationalization of industries or other seizures of assets.

FIGURE 2.7 COMPARISON OF INVESTMENTS USING THE PAYBACK METHOD

	Investment	Annual Yield	Years of Return	Years for Payback	Total Income
Deal A	$250,000	$50,000	7	5	$350,000
Deal B	250,000	50,000	10	5	500,000

KEY FINANCIAL RATIOS

We can learn a great deal about an organization by compiling ratios culled from its financial statements. These ratios are strong indicators of the organization's solvency (i.e., ability to meet its financial obligations), efficiency, or profitability. While the standards (i.e., what is regarded as "good" or "bad") for some ratios may apply across industry lines, they do tend to differ by industry. To find guidelines or parameters on an industry-specific basis, the following sources can probably be found in the reference section of your business library:

Dun & Bradstreet, *Industry Norms and Key Business Ratios* (New York: Dun & Bradstreet, 1992).

Troy Almanac of Business and Industrial Financial Ratios (Englewood Cliffs, NJ: Prentice Hall, 1992).

Robert Morris & Associates, *Annual Statement Studies* (Philadelphia: RMA, annual).

To find a "one-stop" source of 200 "generic" business ratios, I refer to:

Michael R. Tyran, *The Vest-Pocket Guide to Business Ratios* (Englewood Cliffs, NJ: Prentice Hall, 1992).

Personally, I have found the following formulas to be particularly important (and apply them to the financial statements for Your Company, Inc.):[1]

Working Capital or Current Ratio

The working capital or current ratio (see the balance sheet in Figure 2.1) is a measure of short-term solvency, in relative terms. The formula that expresses this is:

$$\text{Working capital} = \frac{\text{Current assets}}{\text{Current liabilities}}$$

Placing the values from the balance sheet (Figure 2.1) into the formula yields:

$$\text{Working capital} = \frac{\$39 \text{ million}}{\$47 \text{ million}} = 0.83$$

Generally, the ratio should be greater than 1:1. Your Company's current ratio is only 0.83. So the firm might attempt to restructure its debt, deferring some of it further into the future (see debt-to-equity ratio, which follows).

Net Working Capital

Net working capital (see balance sheet in Figure 2.1) is a measure of short-term solvency, in absolute terms (i.e., dollars). Although it is not in strict terms a ratio, it is a practical indicator of likely creditworthiness, since banks and other lending institutions typically require certain minimum levels of net working capital. The formula that expresses this is:

Net working capital = Current assets − current liabilities

Placing the values from the balance sheet (Figure 2.1) into the formula yields:

Net working capital = $39 million − $47 million = −$8 million

Your Company's net working capital is −$8 million, a negative figure. So the firm may have to generate capital by other means, such as selling its assets or stock.

Incidentally, one of the most common causes of new business failure is undercapitalization. Fledgling enterprises with solid product lines and good marketing efforts may nonetheless require a great deal of funding, especially in capital-intensive industries, such as manufacturing.

Liquidity Ratio or Quick Ratio

The liquidity ratio or quick ratio (see balance sheet in Figure 2.1) is another measure of short-term solvency, in relative terms. It is a conservative indicator, given that the assets represented in the numerator of the ratio do not include inventory, which is difficult to liquidate quickly. The formula that expresses this is:

$$\text{Liquidity ratio} = \frac{\text{Cash, accounts receivable, marketable securities}}{\text{Current liabilities}}$$

Placing the values from the balance sheet (Figure 2.1) into the formula yields:

$$\text{Liquidity ratio} = \frac{\$22.5 \text{ million}}{\$47.0 \text{ million}} = 0.48$$

Your Company's quick ratio is only approximately 0.48. This ratio should always be greater than 1:1. It can even be as high as 4:1 (sometimes even higher, depending upon the industry).

Debt-to-Equity Ratio

The debt-to-equity ratio (see balance sheet in Figure 2.1) is a measure of long-term solvency, in relative terms. The formula that expresses this is:

$$\text{Debt-to-equity ratio} = \frac{\text{Total liabilities}}{\text{Total shareholders' equity}}$$

Placing the values from the balance sheet (Figure 2.1) into the formula yields:

$$\text{Debt-to-equity ratio} = \frac{\$80 \text{ million}}{\$145 \text{ million}} = 0.55$$

Generally speaking, the debt-to-equity ratio should be less than 0.80. Your Company's debt-to-equity ratio is approximately 55 percent. Not bad. So this figure suggests that the firm might possibly be able to "trade off" its long-term obligations against its short-term obligations (by renegotiating the terms of loan repayment, for example).

Incidentally, indebtedness or leverage is not a bad thing per se. In fact, it can be said that a firm with absolutely no debt is not optimally managed. To use a point of reference in our personal financial lives: Buying a home for cash is not generally as advantageous as taking a loan to finance the purchase, since the mortgage payments are tax deductible and can be paid from future earnings. This, in effect, reduces the initial cash outflow.

Operating Profit Margin

Operating profit margin (see income statement in Figure 2.2) is a measure of profitability before interest charges and taxes, in relative terms. The formula that expresses this is:

$$\text{Operating profit margin} = \frac{\text{Operating income}}{\text{Sales}}$$

Placing the values from the income statement (Figure 2.2) into the formula yields:

$$\text{Operating profit margin} = \frac{\$14 \text{ million}}{\$100 \text{ million}} = 0.14$$

The standard may vary by industry. For example, 5 percent might be the norm for supermarket chains, whereas 40 percent might be more appropriate for cable TV multisystem operators.

Inventory Turnover

Inventory turnover (see balance sheet in Figure 2.1) is a measure of efficiency. The higher, the better. The formula that express this is:

$$\text{Inventory turnover} = \frac{\text{Total inventory}}{\text{Average level of inventory}}$$

Using the values from the balance sheet (Figure 2.1) and assuming that the average level of inventory is 1.65 (since that figure is not presented in the financial statements), the formula yields:

$$\text{Inventory turnover} = \frac{\$16.5 \text{ million}}{\$1.65 \text{ million}} = 10\times$$

The standard differs by industry. Low turnover may suggest a non-competitive or obsolescent product. However, low turnover is not necessarily bad. For example, art galleries that deal in high-priced, high-margin items may sell their entire inventory of extremely expensive paintings at auction only once or twice a year.

Sales-to-Employees Ratio

The sales-to-employees ratio (see income statement in Figure 2.2) is a measure of efficiency. It may implicitly indicate the extent to which an organization is automated. Or it might suggest the skill level of the organization's sales (and marketing) personnel. The formula that expresses this is:

$$\text{Sales-to-employees ratio} = \frac{\text{Sales}}{\text{Number of employees}}$$

Using the values from the income statement (Figure 2.2) and assuming that the number of employees is 500 (since that figure is not presented in these particular financial statements), the formula yields:

$$\text{Sales-to-employees ratio} = \frac{\$100 \text{ million}}{500 \text{ employees}} = \$200{,}000 \text{ per employee}$$

The higher the ratio, the better, so long as the customer focus orientation is not diminished.

Return on Assets

Return on assets or ROA (see balance sheet and income statement, Figures 2.1 and 2.2) is a key measure of management productivity, an indicator of how well the firm's assets are being utilized.

The formula that expresses this is:

$$\text{Return on assets} = \frac{\text{Net income}}{\text{Assets}}$$

Placing the values from the balance sheet (Figure 2.1) and income statement (Figure 2.2) into the formula yields:

$$\text{Return on assets} = \frac{\$8.5 \text{ million}}{\$225.0 \text{ million}} = 0.037$$

Your Company's ROA is 3.7 percent. The standard for ROA varies by industry. Some years ago, an accountant hired by Universal Pictures was escorted to the lot where many of the company's feature films were shot. As the story has it, he found the movie set very exciting. He asked his host/new boss what was done with the studio set when films were not actually in production only to be informed that the gates were locked and security guards posted to prevent theft and vandalism. The new hire then suggested that it would make a fascinating tour for vacationers and other visitors (creative management thinking). And that suggestion gave birth to what we know today as the famous Universal Tour.

Another entertainment industry story: As a young man working for his family's funeral parlor business, Steven J. Ross noticed that the limousines used for funeral services laid idle in the evenings. So he arranged for a livery service to hire the vehicles during what would otherwise have been considered "downtime." It was this type of resourcefulness and astute deployment of assets that enabled Ross to grow a small car rental business, merge it with a garage firm (and the family's funeral parlor business), and acquire a motion picture and record company, transforming this entity into Warner Communications and, ultimately, Time Warner, Inc.[2]

Return on Equity

Return on equity or ROE (see balance sheet and income statement in Figures 2.1 and 2.2) is a key measure of profitability. The formula that expresses this is:

$$\text{Return on equity} = \frac{\text{Net income}}{\text{Shareholders' equity}}$$

Placing the values from the balance sheet (Figure 2.1) and income statement (Figure 2.2) into the formula yields:

$$\text{Return on equity} = \frac{\$8.5 \text{ million}}{\$145.0 \text{ million}} = 0.059$$

Your Company's ROE is 5.9 percent. The standard for ROE varies by industry. The higher, the better. However, the investor may weigh an organization's ROE against the yields of "passive" investment options (e.g., money markets or commercial paper) or those of other "active" investment options.

Return on Investment

Return on investment or ROI (see balance sheet and income statement) is a key measure of profitability, relative to the firm's basic operations, an indicator of what management guru Peter Drucker would characterize as management's effectiveness ("doing the right things") and efficiency ("doing things right"). The formula that expresses this is:

$$\text{Return on investment} = \frac{\text{Operating income}}{\text{Assets}}$$

Placing the values from the balance sheet (Figure 2.1) and income statement (Figure 2.2) into the formula yields:

$$\text{Return on investment} = \frac{\$14 \text{ million}}{\$225 \text{ million}} = 0.062$$

Your Company's ROI is 6.2 percent. Although the standards vary by industry, ROI yields of 0 to 10 percent are generally viewed as low, 10 to 20 percent as medium, and anything in excess of 20 percent as high. Note: Analysts differ as to the "proper" formula for ROI. Some prefer to use "net income" as the numerator (i.e., a more conservative indicator), while others prefer to use "operating income." Similarly, analysts interested in long-range funding might tend to favor "assets minus current liabilities" as the denominator, rather than "assets."[3] In this sense, the definition of the formula is subjective and open to interpretation.

Price-to-Earnings Ratio

P/E is a key measure of profitability, particularly from an investor's perspective. The formula that expresses this is:

$$P/E = \frac{\text{Price per share of common stock}}{\text{Earnings per share (EPS) of common stock*}}$$

So, if we have net income of $8.5 million and we have 4.25 million shares of common stock outstanding, we have EPS of $2. If the price of a share is $30, then the P/E is 15. High-growth industries tend to have higher P/E, because higher earnings are anticipated in the future.

LEASE VERSUS BUY VERSUS RENT

Lease/buy/rent decisions are made on the basis of five criteria (see Figure 2.8): cash flow, commitment, cost, tax impact, and obsolescence risk.

Cash Flow

When we buy (i.e., cash price), our cash flow is immediately and adversely affected, equivalent to the purchase price. To lease or rent, in contrast, involves outgoing cash flow in smaller payments over time.

Commitment

When we buy, we are "locked in" to the purchase (unless, of course we have bought on a trial basis and can return the item within a limited time period). Lease arrangements may allow us to terminate the deal.

---

*EPS = net income divided by the number of common stock shares.

FIGURE 2.8   LEASE/BUY/RENT DECISIONS

	Buy	Lease	Rent
Cash Flow	−	+	+
Commitment	−	−	+
Cost	+	−	?
Tax Impact	+	Closed end + Open end	+
Obsolesence Risk	−	+	+

However, the penalties usually incurred do not make it worthwhile to do so. Rental suggests no commitment. (One can rent day to day or month to month, etc.)

Cost

With the time value of money as a factor, buying is actually less expensive than leasing, since the latter involves interest built in to installment payments. Rental may or may not be cost effective, depending on the nature of usage. For example, rental of tables and chairs for a once-a-year "season's greetings" party might justify rental, whereas regular daily usage of an automobile by a sales representative would probably not.

Tax Impact

With purchases and leases, the transaction would allow for depreciation and the potential for reduced tax liability. Rentals are not depreciated but can be deducted as expenses nonetheless.

Obsolescence Risk

As this relates to commitment, purchases do not allow us to exchange the item for a newer, better version. However, leases often do. And rentals provide a great deal of flexibility to upgrade or switch.

FUNDING

Sources

Simply put, capital (along with talent, of course) is the fuel that runs the business enterprise. To the extent that growth is sought, fuel must be expended. It is interesting to note that a large percentage of business start-ups fail not because of poor general management skills or the lack of product integrity, but rather as a result of inadequate funding. In fact, many would-be entities never materialize at all due to such inability. The irony is that there are many excellent sources that go virtually untapped, often because a surprising number of those who seek funding are not even aware that they exist, much less how to approach them. These sources include the following:

Self

Entrepreneurs can tap their bank accounts, securities, insurance policies, and retirement plans and draw upon their home equity in the form of loans as well. While this may be an easily accessible source for many individuals, the magnitude of the potential risk is great for the individuals and their families. (What will happen if I lose my home?)

Family and Friends

Gifts, loans, or equity involving loved ones as a source are also easily accessible for many individuals. Once again, however, doing business with loved ones may hold the potential for risks of the emotional variety. (If the deal goes sour, will my relative/friend and I still be on good terms, or will it damage the relationship?)

Informal Private Investors (IPI)

This is a popular way to fund various enterprises. In fact, some industries or fields of endeavor rely heavily on IPIs, such as Broadway and the theatrical world with its ad hoc syndicates of funding "angels," who acquire equity interests in plays. While angels may be capable of underwriting the venture, they do not generally offer expertise in addition to their capital.

Suppliers (of Goods or Services)

Suppliers commonly extend trade credit to fledgling business enterprises. Also, they may be candidates for barter arrangements, wherein you would receive their goods or services in return for your goods or services. "Taking a percentage in trade" is a common practice in the service sector. Certain industries, such as media, advertising, restaurant/hotel/hospitality, and equipment rental are heavily dependent upon barter. Barter exchanges or service organizations link traders in return for annual "membership" fees plus a small percentage of the cash value of each transaction that is arranged. (It should be noted that, under the regulations of the Internal Revenue Service, barter transactions are taxable just as cash transactions are.)

Employees

Some of the folks on your payroll might actually be eager to invest in the firm. The employee with an equity stake has an incentive to be more productive. Also, this funding approach allows the employer to tap a source of low-cost capital. The key consideration may be the extent to which owners are willing to relinquish equity and control.

Sellers (of Business Enterprises)

This category represents a largely untapped source of funding and, for that matter, of finding a business to purchase and operate. There are a great many small and small-to-midsized companies (i.e., $500,000 to $5 million) that are forced to liquidate because their owners are ill, wish to retire, or simply have no heirs or successors to take over upon their demise. These enterprises typically are liquidated for 15 to 20 percent of their true value. Such situations present a perfect opportunity for those who wish to buy a business for little or no money down.

Licensees

An organization may be able to raise capital by licensing rights to its product or service. This may be on a limited basis, such as the exclusive right to offer the product or service in a foreign country. There is virtually no direct or immediate cost involved in granting licenses. However, it may be difficult to "police" the licensee. As a result, the integrity of the product or service and, ultimately, the reputation of the licenser may be jeopardized.

Customers

Clients or patrons may help to capitalize enterprises in a variety of ways, perhaps without even realizing that they are doing so. In the early days of the home video rental industry, entrepreneurs typically charged customers a "membership" fee of $25 to $100. That fee actually financed the purchase of video programs/movies that these "members" later rented. Similarly, many direct mail entrepreneurs order their merchandise only after receiving payment in advance from customers. Discounts can be offered as further inducements toward this end.

Banks

Commercial loans may be a viable alternative. However, the cost of capital may be high, and the bank may place certain restrictions on the borrower. Then, again, money may be tight and application by a new enterprise (without a substantial credit history) may be declined.

Government

States and municipalities operate business development units with the express purpose of luring business. They can arrange for substantial

tax breaks, free or very inexpensive facilities, labor, and other direct or indirect funding. The federal government provides loans through its Small
Business Administration (SBA) and awards outright grants through its
other agencies. Of course, foreign governments offer similar inducements
to attract commercial activity.

Venture Capital

Unlike most other investors, venture capitalists are generally "dedicated" professionals, whose sole activity is funding business enterprises
in return for equity positions. They may command a large minority or
even a majority interest in the organization. In addition to providing capital, however, they often bring to the table many years of specialized experience in a particular industry along with numerous valuable contacts.

Corporate Underwriting/Alliance

This is essentially a joint venture or partnership with a large corporation. Funding may only be one of several important advantages offered
by the partner. Others may include access to markets, sales representation, and sophisticated support for research and development.

Initial Public Offering (IPO)

The organization may be able to raise a great deal of money by
"going public," selling shares in the corporation through the stock market. This is often done as an over-the-counter (OTC) issue. However, the
legal costs involved in filing typically run well into six figures. So the
amount one wishes to raise should be substantial relative to these costs.

Partial Public Subsidiary (PPS)

Taking an organization's subsidiary public is not an option for small
organizations. However, the opportunity provides inexpensive equity
capital. It also tends to increase motivation of the subsidiary's employees.
The poorer the performance of the subsidiary prior to going PPS, the
more likely it is to succeed as one.

Leveraged Buyout (LBO)

Leveraged buyouts (LBOs) are purchase arrangements that involve more debt and less equity than is commonly accepted to finance a business purchase.

This investment increases the assumption of risk, because the heavy interest expense serves to reduce future net income. If future earnings can't cover repayment of the debt, the organization may be forced into bankruptcy. Common approaches to LBO include the issuance of "junk bonds" that offer the potential of high yields to offset the risk.

Documentation

The submission of *pro forma statements* to potential investors is standard practice. These documents include assumed or projected figures or facts. In addition to employing pro forma materials to gauge an investment opportunity objectively, savvy investors may also use these as indirect indicators of just how realistic or candid and trustworthy the management team really is. Figure 2.9 provides a suggested outline for presentation of pro forma statements.

SOME TIPS

It should be noted that I am momentarily going "off the record." The following information or advice may be very helpful if you are trying to get an enterprise or project funded. However, it is not generally covered within the MBA curriculum.

Adler's Laws

The noted venture capitalist Fred Adler once posited:

- The size of the CEO's office is inversely related to the likelihood of the business' success. Lavish spending is decidedly not a plus.
- The amount of publicity preceding formal launch of an enterprise is inversely related to the likelihood of its success. From the competitors' perspective, to be forewarned is to be forearmed.

FIGURE 2.9   SAMPLE COVER SHEET AND TABLE OF
              CONTENTS FOR A PRO FORMA
              STATEMENT

(Cover Sheet)

**A BUSINESS PLAN
FOR
YOUR COMPANY, INC.
ANYTOWN, ANYSTATE**

Jane Doe
President
(999) 555-5555

or

A FINANCING PROPOSAL

Submitted to

Last National Bank
of Anytown

by

**YOUR COMPANY, INC.
ANYTOWN, ANYSTATE**

Jane Doe
President
(999) 555-5555

FIGURE 2.9   (Continued)

Table of Contents

STATEMENT OF PURPOSE

I   THE BUSINESS
Description of the Business
Market and Competition Analysis
Products
Services
Manufacturing and Service Delivery Facilities/Operations
Location
Marketing Plan
Future Change Strategies
Management Team
Operating Personnel
Venture Development Schedule
Proposed Uses of Funds Requested
Critical Risks and Problems
Summary

II   FINANCIAL DATA
Sources and Applications of Funds
Capital Equipment List
Pro Forma Balance Sheet as of Commencement of Business
Break-even Analysis

PRO FORMA INCOME FORECASTS
Three-Year Summary
Detail by Month, Year 1
Detail by Quarter, Years 2 and 3
Notes of Explanation

PRO FORMA CASH FLOW ANALYSIS
Three-Year Summary
Detail by Month, Year 1
Detail by Quarter, Years 2 and 3
Notes of Explanation

PRO FORMA BALANCE SHEETS
By Quarter, Year 1
Annual, Years 2 and 3

III   PRODUCTS AND SERVICES
Appendix I   Product and Service Program Outlines
Appendix II   Marketing Plan
Appendix III   Background of Principal(s)
Appendix IV   Material Resources and Operations

Sobel's Suggestions

Though I am not a venture capitalist or a highly sophisticated investor, I have given my students and consulting clients the following advice and am told that it was helpful:

- When a prospective investor agrees to meet with you and asks what time is good for you, request before 7:00 A.M. or after 8:00 P.M. You are likely to be met with either of two responses: the individual will express shock that you want to meet so early or so late. This provides you with the perfect opportunity to explain that you put in very long hours. This indicates your seriousness of purpose and commitment to the business.

- When you take a meal at a restaurant with a potential investor, don't be quick to pick up the check. That does not mean that you shouldn't pick up the check, only that you shouldn't be eager to do so (unless, of course, you specifically invited the investor to be your guest). Eagerness to pay the tab may be construed as spendthrift behavior (not good). Moreover, your willingness to gain favor may also welcome more requests or demands for concessions than you would otherwise need to grant.

THE ACCOUNTING AND FINANCE CHECKLIST

1. Can I take greater advantage of tax reduction strategies?
2. Can I do more to improve my internal control procedures to better safeguard my assets?
3. Is my current cash flow strategy optimal or can it be improved?
4. Have I calculated key ratios to compare my company's performance to others in the same industry?
5. Have I chosen the best investment options?
6. Should other or additional funding sources be identified and considered?

RECOMMENDED READING

Boutell, Wayne S., *Accounting for Anyone* (Englewood Cliffs, NJ: Prentice Hall, 1982).

Donnahoe, Alan, *What Every Manager Should Know About Financial Analysis* (New York: Fireside/Simon & Schuster, 1989).

Finkler, Steven A., *Finance & Accounting for Nonfinancial Managers* (Englewood Cliffs, NJ: Prentice Hall, 1992).

Merrill, Ronald E., and Gaylord E. Nichols, *Raising Money* (New York: AMACOM, 1990).

Peterson, Robert C., *Understanding Accounting—Fast* (New York: McGraw-Hill, 1976).

ORGANIZATIONS AND RESOURCES

American Institute of Certified Public Accountants
1211 Avenue of the Americas
New York, New York 10036
(212) 575-6200

National Association of Accountants
10 Paragon Drive
Montvale, NJ 07645
(201) 573-9000

American Finance Association
100 Trinity Place (N.Y.U.)
New York, New York 10006
(212) 285-8915

Angel Networks
(MIT Enterprise Forum)
201 Vassar Street
Cambridge, MA 02139
(617) 253-8240

Financial Managers Society
111 S. Wacker Drive
Chicago, IL 60601
(312) 938-2576

National Corporate Cash Management Association
7315 Wisconsin Avenue (Suite 1250)
Bethesda, MD 20814
(301) 907-2862

National Venture Capital Association
1655 N. Fort Myer Drive
Arlington, VA 22209
(703) 528-4370

ENDNOTES

1. All ratios except ROI are from Michael R. Tyran, *The Vest-Pocket Guide to Business Ratios* (Englewood Cliffs, NJ: Prentice Hall, 1992).
2. Roger Cohen, "The Creator of Time Warner, Steven J. Ross, Is Dead at 65," *The New York Times,* December 21, 1992, pp. D1 and D12.
3. W. W. Cooper and Yuri Ijiri (eds.), *Kohler's Dictionary for Accountants* (Englewood Cliffs, NJ: Prentice Hall, 1983).

CHAPTER 3

HUMAN RESOURCES AND OPERATIONS MANAGEMENT

HUMAN RESOURCES MANAGEMENT

Human resources management (HRM) is concerned with maximizing employee competency and motivation, the desired end being enhanced productivity. Let us review the history or evolution of the discipline.

Pre-Scientific Era (–1910)

HRM has been traced as far back as the eighteenth century B.C., to the Code of Hammurabi and the establishment of what we regard today as a minimum wage. More complex compensation structures began to emerge following the Arsenal of Venice in 1436, which distinguished between per diem and piecework rates, depending upon the nature of work performed.

Scientific Management Era (1910–1940)

Early in the twentieth century, Frederick Taylor (1911) introduced the so-called *scientific approach to management* and, along with it, the intention of establishing management as a discrete field of endeavor, "professionalizing" the discipline. In fact, it was during this period that the term "efficiency expert" came into being. Emphasis was on improving the task. Toward this end, time-and-motion studies were introduced to eliminate any extraneous steps involved.

In 1916, Henri Fayol introduced the *process approach*. This is characterized by a shift in emphasis from improving the worker's performance of tasks to developing management's skills.

This was followed in 1927 by the work of Elton Mayo. His *Hawthorne studies*, which were conducted at a Western Electric plant in Hawthorne, California, indicated that workers' productivity did not decline despite adverse physical working conditions. They realized the importance of their participation in the experiment, underscoring the role of motivation toward productivity.[1]

Human Relations Era (1940–1960)

Perhaps the hallmark of this period is the *hierarchy of needs model* advanced by Abraham Maslow in 1954 (see Figure 3.1). This concept emphasizes that employees (actually, any individuals, vocationally or avocationally) may be at differing levels of attainment or need at different points in their lives.[2] So it is implicit that the enlightened manager identify each subordinate's level of attainment within the context of a hierarchy of needs and motivate him or her toward greater productivity on an individualized basis.

There are two basic limitations of the model. First, it assumes that as a "lower" need is met, a "higher" need is amplified. While this may technically be true, it suggests that the satisfaction of needs is sequential when, in fact, it is concurrent. An individual may have satisfied the self-esteem need although the safety need has not yet been satisfied. Second, it assumes that the pecking order of this sequence is accurate and universally applicable. Clearly, culture makes a difference. While a typical American of European descent is likely to more readily satisfy

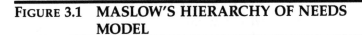

FIGURE 3.1   MASLOW'S HIERARCHY OF NEEDS MODEL

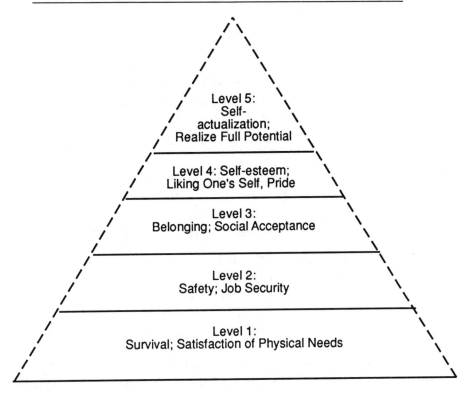

the survival need before the self-actualization need, the reverse might be true of the typical Indian, who might realize full potential although he or she is starving to death.

Managers may employ the following "motivators" to help satisfy needs:

Level 1: Survival   Raise in salary
                             Bonus
                             Better working conditions
                             Periodic medical examinations
                             Recreation

Level 2: Safety	Stock options
	Insurance
	Tenure
	Verbal and written acknowledgment
	Promotions
Level 3: Belonging	Invitation to special events
	Task force opportunities
	Committee opportunities
	Membership in organizational "clubs"
	Transfers
Level 4: Self-esteem	Awards
	Letters of commendation
	Titles
	Publicity exposure
	Serve on management council
Level 5: Self-actualization	Sabbatical leaves
	Leading task forces
	Educational opportunities
	Teaching assignments
	Coaching assignments[3]

In 1960, Douglas McGregor introduced the concepts of *Theory X and Theory Y*, the former indicative of an autocratic management style and the latter indicative of an egalitarian management style.[4] Based upon our assumptions of human behavior, all of us have some kind of management style, whether or not we know it or wish to acknowledge it. The autocratic and custodial management styles reflect the Theory X mind-set, whereas the participative and collegial management styles reflect the Theory Y mind-set (see Figure 3.2).

Humanistic Psychology Era (1960–1970)

During this decade, V. H. Vroom, Porter and Lawler, and others wrote extensively about *expectancy theory*, maintaining that management can effectively motivate workers toward desired goals by providing

FIGURE 3.2   MANAGEMENT STYLES

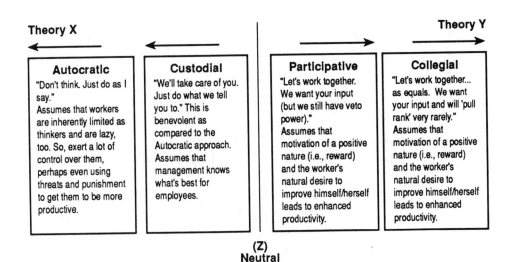

appropriate incentives. In a similar vein, Lawrence and Lorsch and others wrote about *contingency theory*, asserting that there is no "one best way" or single style of management that would be suitable on a universal or generalized basis; it all depends upon the particular situation. This would not even preclude the so-called *KITA approach*, an acronym for Kick In The Ass. Herzberg, who introduced the term, suggests that even "nice guys [and gals]" sometimes have to adopt a harsher management style in order to deal with a particular type of worker or work condition.[5]

How can we gauge management or work style relative to personality type? Perhaps the most widely used measurement tool for this purpose is the *Myers-Briggs Type Inventory® (MBTI)*. It is based upon Carl Jung's *theory of psychological profiles* and relies upon self-reported preferences in terms of 4 personality dimensions (see Figure 3.3), which allow for 16 permutations or possible personality types:

1. Interaction with the environment (*extraverted*) in contrast to quiet reflection (*introverted*)

2. Conceptual approach coupled with "gut" feelings (*intuitive*) in contrast to experiential approach with "here and now" orientation (*sensing*)

3. Emphasis on personal values (*feeling*) in contrast to practical and objective considerations or "what will work" (*thinking*)

4. Open-end exploration (*perceiving*) in contrast to decisions and closure (*judging*)[6]

This enables the test taker to gain insights regarding inclinations and associated strengths and weaknesses. It might seem that individuals who share the same or similar type are likely to get along better than those who do not. However, getting along and working together productively is another matter entirely. In fact, the complement of opposite types is probably very healthy, and MBTI allows dissimilar individuals to understand each other better and work together more effectively. Some critics of MBTI view the test as a means of typecasting individuals so that they are precluded from consideration for opportunities based solely upon their profile. (For this reason, it can reasonably be argued that it should not be used as an appraisal tool by management, only confidentially by the individual for his or her own insights.) Others contend that since MBTI is based upon self-reported assessments, the lack of objectivity or bias may render the test invalid. Moreover, participants may rationalize the findings if they don't like the implications. And most interesting and controversial is the assertion that individual personality plays a very small role as a determinant of group performance.

Management by objective (MBO), developed by George S. Odiorne, came into widespread usage during the same general period that MBTI was introduced. MBO is intended to provide a framework for planning the tasks an employee is expected to perform and the goals

FIGURE 3.3   MYERS-BRIGGS TYPE INVENTORY®

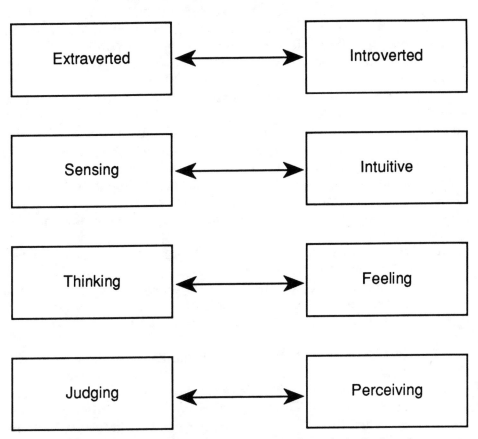

Source: Jean M. Kummerow, *Verifying Your Type Preferences,* Center for Applications of Psychological Type, Gainsville, FL, 1987

that individual is expected to achieve within a particular time frame. Theoretically, the manager will meet with the subordinate, and together they will discuss and jointly decide what the subordinate will be expected to accomplish within the upcoming business period. So it can be said that the MBO ostensibly provides the opportunity for agreement and for documentation of such agreement as this relates to accountability.[7]

In practice, however, the MBO is all too often abused. For example, a manager might try to flatter or coerce the subordinate into "signing off" on tasks or objectives that are unreasonable or unattainable or that the subordinate is otherwise unwilling to perform or actualize. Moreover, circumstances beyond the subordinate's control that prevent successful completion are not necessarily factored into evaluation of performance.

Even more troubling, though, is the potential for portions of the MBO to be purposefully interpreted out of context to undermine the subordinate's subsequent appraisal. For example, the MBO may include a seemingly innocuous question, such as *"What skills would you like to improve?"* At the time of appraisal, the manager may try to justify a poor (and unfair) evaluation by claiming that the subordinate lacked certain skills . . . that the individual even implicitly conceded in the MBO. For these reasons, abuse of the MBO has been referred to as *management by terror (MBT)*.

(It is interesting to note that a few companies have begun to use the *"reverse review"* method of performance appraisal, which essentially enables employees to evaluate their bosses. Of course, employee confidentiality must be protected. This approach is consistent with participative management style. In addition to providing feedback from the "bottom up," it can give employees a "voice" and a greater sense of empowerment.)

Systems Era (1980–   )

This period is almost synonymous with the theme of *total quality management (TQM)*. The cornerstones of TQM include a striving toward constant and ongoing improvement, setting long-term objectives, empowering employees, and utilizing the team approach.

Although the preeminent TQM "gurus" may differ over how it can be accomplished, all seem to agree that it is critical to "do it right the first time" and to satisfy and perhaps even surpass the expectations of clients. Aside from the fact that "doing it right the first time" is congruent with a customer-focus orientation, it often costs a great deal more to correct or undo an error than to avoid making it in the first place. TQM guru Philip Crosby places this cost at approximately one quarter of total revenues.

Benchmarking is a popular concept in the TQM world. Simply put, managers are encouraged to observe the ways that their counterparts in other organizations can shed light on how they themselves can improve performance in their own organizations. As you might imagine, competitors are not likely to be sharing with one another. However, it may very well be appropriate for managers in allied or unrelated industries. Etiquette dictates that you should be willing to reveal the same type of information that you request from your counterparts.

A frequent phenomenon associated with TQM is *reduced cycle time.* By minimizing mistakes and turnaround time in production situations, for example, a manufacturing run can be completed more quickly and the product can be brought to market sooner. In a similar vein, adding value or utility to tasks is also stressed. Toward this end, one of Motorola's quality experts is said to have the following outgoing message on his voice mail (to paraphrase): "If speaking with me will add value for you or for me, leave a message. If not, hang up now."

It is no surprise that much of the tremendous success of Japan's manufacturing is attributable to TQM efforts. It is ironic, however, in light of America's relatively lackluster performance, that TQM as we know it was introduced to the Japanese many years ago by an American, W. Edwards Deming. In fact, Deming is so revered in Japan that the country's most prestigious award for quality control, the Deming Prize, was established in his honor more than 40 years ago by the Japanese Union of Scientists and Engineers. In addition, eligibility for the Japan Quality Control Award, which was established almost 30 years later, is limited to winners of the Deming Prize. Deming, who is close to 90 years old now, has long enjoyed the reputation of a curmudgeon, purportedly refusing to continue working with executives who fail to learn as quickly as he would like. The key points of Deming's platform are:[8]

- Drive out fear.
- Get rid of numerical goals (e.g., quotas).

- Train on the job (OJT).
- Deemphasize short-term profits.

Over the past decade or so, Philip Crosby has popularized the term *zero defects* as a quality control orientation. This approach calls for 100 percent error-free performance as a goal. Crosby contends that to establish any level of defects as "acceptable" tends to have the effect of making that level (or higher) a self-fulfilling prophecy; if employees know that it is "okay" to operate at a certain error level, they will come to view the level as a "standard." Of course, this standard is suboptimal.[9]

The story is told of Crosby attending his daughter's lavish wedding and abstaining from indulging in even a single celebratory alcoholic toast. His explanation: zero defects. He was on a diet at the time and to depart from his regimen, even for a special occasion, would constitute a ZD lapse.

A caveat involves cross-cultural perceptions of ZD, insofar as it may be used as a "selling point" to prospective customers. In certain cultures, error-free performance is an alien concept and inconsistent with a belief system that generously factors in human fallibility. So, while zero defects policies enable organizations to satisfy their customers better, it is ironic that communication of this approach to customers does not necessarily go over as well as expected.

A contemporary of Deming, Joseph Juran, liberally expanded the definition of "customer" to include internal entities, such as coworkers. When coworker A passes the unfinished product to coworker B on the production line, coworker B becomes coworker A's "customer." Actually, any coworker or individual within the organization who can be helped or served by other employees may be regarded as their "customer." Juran emphasized the value of problem-solving and brainstorming teams. Unlike Deming, however, he contended that *fear can be a positive motivating influence.*[10]

In 1981, William Ouchi espoused the notion of *Theory Z*, the melding of American and Japanese management styles (perhaps also an amalgam of McGregor's Theory X and Theory Y). He promoted substantive involvement in quality control at all levels of management and work force, understanding of broader organizational objectives, reduced division of labor, and profit sharing.[11]

DIMENSIONS OF MANAGERIAL EFFECTIVENESS

It is difficult to generalize about the components of managerial effectiveness, because many of the necessary skills are "soft" and subjective and difficult to assess. These include leadership, motivation, people skills, and administrative/strategic skills.

Leadership

At the very least, managers must be able to exert their authority. Ideally, subordinates will follow a manager's directives solely on the basis of their respect for that individual's personal integrity and/or professional attainment rather than the formal authority that accompanies a title. In this sense, it can be said that the best of managers lead by example, providing role models for their staffs. As I reflect on leaders that I have worked for or worked with, one in particular comes to mind as extraordinary. His subordinates respected and admired him to such an extent that, in the face of a less than excellent performance on their part, they would immediately express concern about how this might affect their boss. (The vast majority of employees would, of course, focus instead on their own self-interest.)

Motivation

The best managers make it a point to know what makes their subordinates tick and then to create incentives to get them to be as productive as possible (see Figure 3.1 regarding Maslow's Hierarchy of Needs). This requires managers to wear different hats with different employees at different points in time. An increasingly important aspect of the manager's role involves the training and development of staff. Cultivation of talent is necessary for succession planning and may even be viewed as an entitlement or condition of employment by those who are hired. It is ironic that managers who withhold guidance out of fear that their subordinates might threaten their jobs if they learn too much ultimately threaten their own jobs. These disenchanted employees will probably be less productive or leave for more promising jobs, reflecting poorly on their managers' performance.

People Skills

Diplomacy and "charm" count for a lot. In the corporate world, style may be just as important as substance. One of my senior colleagues, an extremely successful management consultant and keen observer of top executives who are considered for CEO positions, shared with me his empirical finding that the individuals who ascend to the top are not necessarily the best or the brightest. They tend to be nominally competent, but are skillful at getting along with everyone and alienating no one.

Administrative and Strategic Skills

If you manufactured violins and were interviewing for a salesperson, would you hire a violinist and teach him to sell or would you hire a salesperson and teach him to play violin? This question may seem rhetorical, but I assure you, it is commonly posed in corporate boardrooms. John Scully, the chairman of Apple Computers, was recruited from Pepsi-Cola. He had very little knowledge of the computer industry, but he was a "professional manager," the kind that business schools turn out, one who supposedly can manage any type of organization, given that management is a universally applicable skill. Contrast Scully, if you will, with television's "Lou Grant" character, a veteran newsman who knows the particulars of his chosen field "in his sleep." Why didn't Apple bring in a Lou Grant, a computer pro, rather than an industry "outsider" like Scully? Perhaps the Apple board of directors felt that, since the computer industry was maturing, it was no longer necessary to have a "visionary" and computer pro like former Chairman Steven Jobs at the helm. In contrast, Chrysler's board faced considerable criticism when it hired a top executive from General Motors to succeed Chairman Lee Iacocca. The newcomer was a respected automobile pro, yet hiring someone from outside the company was regarded by many as sacrilege. Clearly, the controversy of professional manager versus industry professional will not be resolved here, but it merits further discussion.

WORK VERSUS PLAY

To put it simply, work is not fun and play is (see Figure 3.4). It is only natural that we gravitate toward that which we regard as pleasant or

FIGURE 3.4   WORK VERSUS PLAY

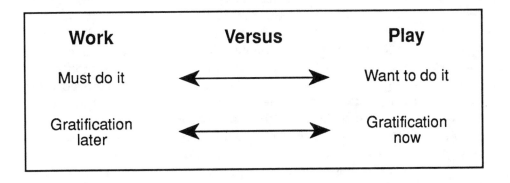

fun. So, to the extent that we must engage in work, the enlightened manager tries to create a work environment that is playlike if not actually playful. Care less about how a job is accomplished, as long as it is completed on time and done well. Give employees the opportunity to make choices whenever possible. After all, it is only fair that if people are to be held responsible for their actions, they also have authority commensurate to the degree of their responsibility. (By the way, considerable responsibility without much authority would explain the feelings of frustration and futility common among many midlevel managers. To paraphrase management guru Tom Peters, "Middle managers are cooked geese. Raise hell and at least go down in flames. You'd be better off getting fired for doing something interesting rather than laid off for doing something boring."[12])

LINE VERSUS STAFF

Line jobs are those with direct authority and profit center orientation, such as sales and production positions. Staff positions support line functions, such as market research and personnel positions. The designation of a particular job in terms of line or staff depends upon the industry. For example, a security officer or specialist employed by Pinkerton would probably be regarded as line, whereas a security officer deployed internally by a bank would probably be regarded as staff. Similarly, a market researcher employed by Nielsen (the folks who conduct television ratings surveys) would probably be regarded as line, whereas a market researcher employed by a manufacturing company would probably be regarded as staff. However, the distinctions are becoming blurred in the midst of a trend toward integration of line and staff. Increasingly, staff people will be assuming responsibility for the profitability of specific accounts, while their line counterparts will be playing more supportive roles that may involve less direct authority.

COMMUNICATION

Since the Tower of Babel, humankind has posted an unimpressive track record in the person-to-person conveyance of information and ideas. I do not believe, even in today's sophisticated business arena, that MBAs necessarily communicate very effectively, or, for that matter, appreciably better (if at all) than their colleagues. Therefore, I will now offer some very basic, practical advice in this area, even though the subject is not generally covered in the MBA curriculum.

Writing Memos

1. Do not write unless it is necessary. Inundating colleagues with "junk memos" is a surefire way to get them angry.

2. Get to the point immediately. Their time is valuable.

3. Be brief.

4. Use simple language.

5. Keep sentences and paragraphs short.

6. Be clear and specific.

7. If you want something, ask for it. It's okay to request action and a reply.

8. Personalize and gear your approach to appeal to the reader's self-interest, not yours. Keep "I" and "my" to a minimum.[13]

Preparing for and Conducting Meetings

1. Clearly establish and state in advance the meeting's objectives and agenda. Distribute pertinent material. This enables participants to prepare properly.

2. Set a time limit.

3. Limit the number of participants to those who can add value and to those who have a stake in the meeting's outcome. Keep in mind that the inclusion of each additional "unnecessary" participant may serve to increase dramatically the likelihood of disagreement (not necessarily a bad thing).

4. Prioritize or rank topics to be addressed. If time constraints are the primary concern, proceed from "most important" to "less important." If agreement is the primary concern, proceed from "most likely to be agreed upon" to "least likely to be agreed upon."

5. To help generate support for your "political" position or cause, it may be appropriate to enter into a dialogue with selected participants privately and in advance.[14]

Negotiating

1. Confirm that the party you are dealing with does, in fact, have the authority to grant you what you want.

2. Begin with those points most likely to be agreed upon, proceeding in descending order.

3. Never give up "something for nothing." Always link something that you are asked to give up with something that you want.

4. Try to see the other person's side.

5. Accept the individual's stated feelings as though they were facts.

6. "Save face" for them if you want them to "give in." Avoid backing people into corners and offending them with phrases like, "Take it or leave it."

7. Periodically repeat and summarize what they are saying, so they will realize that you are taking them seriously and actually listening to them.

8. Let the other party know that you are seeking a "win-win" resolution, so that both parties gain rather than one party winning at the expense of the other.[15]

Giving Praise and Criticism

1. Praise publicly. Making employees look good in front of other coworkers goes a long way toward building positive PR for yourself as well as the obvious recipient of the kind words.

2. Criticize privately. Humiliating an individual in front of others serves no useful purpose, and the damage often cannot be undone.

3. In the immortal words of Lyndon Johnson, "Don't tell 'em to go to hell unless you can send them there."[16]

COMPENSATION

While salary usually comprises the lion's share of a total compensation package, other components have grown in importance so that salary in major corporations comprises only 65 to 75 percent of the compensation pie. The proportions differ by employment stratum, reflecting what is necessary to attract, motivate, and/or keep employees at each level. A recent major criticism involves the contention that distribution of compensation within the corporation is often highly inequitable. In larger corporations, the most senior executive or CEO can earn 70 times more than the employees at the lowest rung of the ladder. (In fact, it was recently disclosed that the CEO of Time Warner earned approximately $80 million in annual compensation, far more than the 70 × multiple.) And to buttress further the claim that large corporations serve the interests of senior management elites, critics need only point out that when senior executives lose their jobs, they often receive "golden parachutes" or generous severance packages while rank-and-file employees can expect to receive far more modest packages.

At the other end of the spectrum, Ben & Jerry's ice cream company represents commitment to industrial democracy, the participation of rank-and-file in decision making and profit participation, including ESOPs, or employee stock ownership plans. Until recently, the company had a policy that precluded the most senior executive from earning more than 5 times the lowest-paid employee. However, as entrepreneurs Ben and Jerry (of Ben & Jerry's Ice Cream) now concede, it became necessary to raise the ratio to 8 to 1 to attract top managerial talent at the "going market rate."

It is particularly interesting to note that much of the compensation of Japanese senior executives is typically deferred until the twilight of their careers, ostensibly to promote long-range decisions (and lower turnover) that are ultimately in the best interests of the organization as well as the executives. American senior executives operate all too often under compensation systems that allow for "quick hits" and relatively immediate gratification. These compensation structures promote short-range decisions wherein the interests of the organization and of its senior management can be mutually exclusive.

LEARNING

Learning is a continuous and ongoing process. The best organizations know this and make substantive commitments to this effort, in three areas: training, education, and development.

Training is learning that is applicable to the individual's current job.

Education is learning that is designed to groom the individual for future jobs he or she may assume.

Development is learning that is geared toward "general growth" of the individual and/or that of the organization and is not directly linked to the person's current position or an identified future job.[17]

The perceived appropriateness of any type of learning program is weighed in terms of its perceived risk and reward. The time lag that occurs between the learning and its observable benefits appears to be a key factor. Management typically is most favorably disposed toward training, since its benefits are observed on the job and short term, if not immediately. Receptivity toward education is often less enthusiastic, since its benefits are generally regarded as midterm. And attitudes toward development tend to be even less positive, since the benefits are viewed as long term and questionable or difficult to measure.

In your role as a successful manager and content expert, you may at some point be called upon to share your considerable knowledge with others in a classroom setting. In anticipation of this, enrolling in a "train-the-trainer" course might be a wise career investment. (You realize, of course, that mastery of the material doesn't necessarily mean that you can teach it well. Just think of the awful instructor or two that you had in college or graduate school.) So, if you have the opportunity to be a learning facilitator (read "instructor") and are unable to attend to "train-the-trainer" program to develop your skills, the following guidelines should be helpful.

Thirty-three Do's of Adult Learning

1. Begin with introductions of yourself and the adult learners.

2. Share some of yourself (i.e., humor, experiences, feelings, self). Be honest, authentic, and self-disclosing.

3. Make sure their first experiences with the subject or class are as positive as possible.

4. Relate learning to adult interests, concerns, and values.

5. Selectively emphasize and deal with the human perspective of what is being learned, with applications to the personal daily lives of the adult learners whenever possible.

6. Use needs assessment techniques to determine the felt needs and actual needs of the learners using assessments administered by the instructor and self-assessments by the adult learner.

7. Provide opportunities for self-directed learning where adults can participate in setting objectives, selecting instructional methods, self-evaluating, and analyzing their performance.

8. Make the learning goals as clear as possible and as appropriate to the learners as possible.

9. Give the rationale for assignments, procedures, and instructional methods.

10. When possible, clearly state or demonstrate the learning that will result from learning activities.

11. Ensure successful learning by planning instructional activities that match the needs and objectives of adult learners.

12. Encourage and challenge the learners.

13. Make learner reaction and active participation an essential part of the learning process.

14. Provide frequent response opportunities for all adult learners on an equitable basis.

15. Promote learners' personal control over the context of learning by involving them in the planning and setting of goals, self-evaluation and determination of their strengths and weaknesses, and recording and analyzing progress.

16. Make the criteria for evaluation as clear as possible.

17. Use consistent feedback to learners regarding their mastery, progress, and responsibility in learning.

18. When it is necessary, use constructive criticism.

19. Effectively use praise and reward learning.

20. Plan with the motivation of the learners in mind. Don't assume that the content or the teacher will maintain their motivation.

21. Create a learning environment that is organized and orderly.

22. Be aware of the needs of adults: their physiological, safety, love and belongingness, and self-esteem needs and curiosity, sense of wonder, and need to explore.

23. Remove or reduce components of learning situations that lead to failure and fear.

24. Introduce the unfamiliar through the familiar.

25. Use unpredictability and uncertainty to the degree that learners enjoy them with a sense of security.

26. Use disequilibrium to stimulate learning by using such methods as contradiction and "leaving them wanting more" and playing the role of the devil's advocate.

27. Use collaboration as an instructional technique to develop and maximize cohesiveness in the group.

28. Create components in the learning environment that tell learners they are accepted respected members of the group.

29. When appropriate, plan activities that allow adults to share and to display publicly their projects and skills.

30. Provide variety in presentational style, methods of instruction, and learning materials.

31. Selectively use breaks, physical exercise, and energizers.

32. Use humor liberally and frequently.

33. Use examples, stories, analogies, and metaphors.[18]

DIVERSITY AND DISCRIMINATION

HRM professionals acknowledge the widespread overrepresentation of white, middle-aged males in the ranks of management. Exclusion of minorities may be subtle or not so subtle. For example, a minority employee can be "promoted" to a position that is either not very visible (and unlikely to showcase the individual's talents) or assigned to one that is doomed to failure. Other variants of the "glass ceiling" may entirely preclude mobility of any substantive kind. While racism and sexism often receive the most attention, other "isms" are no less worthy of our attention. These include discrimination on the basis of age, sexual orientation, and physical or mental disability.

In any event, discrimination in employment is not just against the law. It subjects the employer to possible monetary penalties and damages, as well as adverse publicity. Figuratively speaking, skilled employees (as human capital) are categorized as assets. By failing to deploy these valuable assets properly (or perhaps even driving them from the firm), the manager who discriminates, in effect, devalues the organization's asset base and, therefore, its net worth.

Senior management must, in no uncertain terms, make clear to all employees that discrimination is not acceptable and will not be tolerated. Training programs can be an important component in a more comprehensive plan designed to sensitize employees, to respect one another and perhaps even to celebrate their differences.

CRISIS MANAGEMENT

Given the ever-increasing complexity of the business landscape and the extremely high stakes involved, organizations not only plan to realize their objectives, but they also actively plan to confront their most dreaded possible scenarios.

Crisis management is a specialized area and is to the practice of management what emergency medicine is to the practice of medicine. Both involve the compression of time, and the stakes can be extremely high. The best crisis managers are proactive, anticipating possible catastrophes with various contingency plans to accommodate many scenarios. They have also assembled special task forces that can be sent into action almost without delay. The manager, as spokesperson for the organization, must immediately be prepared to be the source of bad news, rather than the defensive receiver of it, and must reassure customers, constituents, and the general public that their well-being is more important to the company than any profits that may be lost as a result of the catastrophe. Johnson & Johnson did a superb job when its Tylenol® product was tampered with and innocent people died as a result of ingesting the poisoned medication. The company's CEO, James Burke, was very visible from the outset and reassured everyone that extreme measures were already being taken to safeguard lives, and he revealed the specific plans to everyone. His concern for public safety was sincere and convincing.

This is in sharp contrast to Audi's handling of the crisis caused by sudden acceleration of its automobile. The company added insult to injury by blaming the drivers, accusing them of stepping down on the wrong pedal. Similarly, after publicly announcing that some of the chips it had recently manufactured and distributed were defective, Intel Corporation made a terrible error by initially refusing to grant exchanges to all purchasers of the chip. After the public outcry that followed, Intel was forced to grant exchanges to all customers who requested one.

To summarize, the basic tenets of crisis management are:

Anticipation/proactivity

Timely response

Genuine concern

Honesty

Reassurance

OPERATIONS MANAGEMENT

Thus far in this chapter, we have discussed the "soft" skills associated with human behavior in the workplace. In contrast, *operations management (OM)* is comprised largely of "hard" skills and addresses the optimal utilization of materiel, as well as human, resources. OM techniques are crucial in areas such as the production of goods (e.g., assembly-line efficiencies) and the delivery of services (e.g., reducing waiting time for customers). We will examine key concepts and formulas, including economies of scale, crossover analysis, break-even analysis, linear programming, network analysis, queuing theory, and the just-in-time production approach. In this chapter, computation of formulas is generally quite simple, requiring only basic arithmetic skills. The sole exception is for linear programming (LP), which involves an algebraic equation. However, even this formula is reduced to basic arithmetic and presented step by step. And, in practice, LP is virtually always computed by machine.

ECONOMIES OF SCALE

It is important to know the degree to which a larger quantity of units to be produced or purchased will result in a lower average cost per unit (see Figures 3.5 and 3.6). Economies of scale, the cost savings that result from dealing in larger quantities, can be increased to the extent that fixed costs (those not sensitive to variations in volume) are absorbed by each additional unit that is produced or purchased.

FIGURE 3.5   ECONOMIES OF SCALE: THE EFFECT OF QUANTITY ON COST

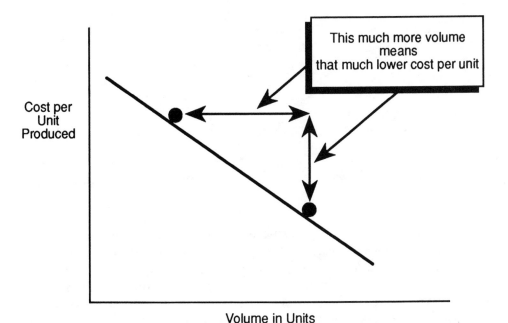

FIGURE 3.6   ECONOMIES OF SCALE: THE EFFECT OF FIXED AND VARIABLE COSTS ON UNIT COSTS

Project A		Project B	
Fixed Cost = $1000		Fixed Cost = $250	
Variable Cost = 5		Variable Cost = 8	

	Unit Cost	
Quantity	Project A	Project B
250	9.00	9.00
500	7.00	8.50
750	6.33	8.33
1000	6.00	8.25
2000	5.50	8.13
5000	5.20	8.05
10000	5.10	8.02

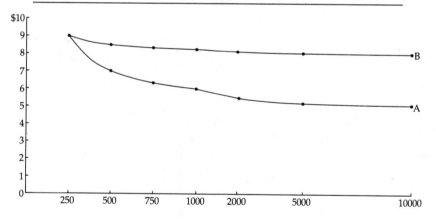

Note: Scale curves, as depictions of economies of scale, are *not* the same as experience curves (also known as learning curves). *Experience curves* reflect situations where costs decrease as experience increases. Thus, the longer we perform a task (given proper training), the better we become at it. We require less time, there are fewer defects or errors made, and, ultimately, costs come down. *Concentration curves* reflect situations where output (productivity) is disproportionate to input (deployment of resources).[19] This is roughly analogous to the 80/20 Rule (see 80/20 Rule discussion later in this chapter).

Assuming that you operate a "fast-food" restaurant, rent, insurance, equipment, furnishings, and utilities are examples of fixed costs, since they do not vary with volume. In other words, they remain pretty much the same regardless of how many orders are filled or how many meals are served. On the other hand, paper cups and napkins are examples of variable costs and are volume sensitive, since the number of these items that are used directly corresponds to the number of drinks that are served. So each additional drink that you serve during a meal period costs less than the one before it, until the economies of scale are exhausted. Moreover, if your restaurant has been open for dinner only, you might entertain the notion of offering lunch as well. After all, your fixed costs (with the exception of an additional shift for your cook, waiters/waitresses, and cashier) would already have been borne. Your variable costs would, in effect, be limited to those associated with food portions actually served.

The most commonly used methods for enhancing economies of scale are mergers and acquisitions, joint ventures, compressed scheduling, and cluster management. We will discuss each method in the context of hospital management.

Mergers and Acquisitions

By consolidating two previously discrete entities into a single one, administrative expenses can often be dramatically reduced. For example, the merger of two hospitals into one would allow the elimination of duplicated efforts (i.e., two human resources departments would not be necessary).

Joint Ventures

If two separate entities are performing the same function and both are operating at a level substantially below full capacity, they can join forces to perform jointly the same function at a level close to full utilization. For example, two neighboring hospitals may decide to share a single CAT SCAN unit.

Compressed Scheduling

Let's assume that a hospital offers a particular outpatient and elective service 8 hours per day for 7 days per week, but actually delivers this service an average of only 5 hours per day. Since demand or utilization is only at about the 62 percent level, it might be more cost effective to close the facility 2 days per week (thereby reducing such costs as labor and utilities), so that service would be provided 7 hours per day for only 5 days per week, near to full utilization.

Cluster Management

If two departments within that hospital are sufficiently related in function (e.g., obstetrics and gynecology), administration might be handled under a single umbrella. Redundancy of labor would be eliminated, and purchasing costs would go down as the result of quantity discounts.

CROSSOVER ANALYSIS

This quantitative tool allows us to determine at what point we should switch from one product or service to a competing option. This relates to economies of scale in that we are dealing with fixed and variable costs.

Example: We can buy a Xerox copying machine for $1,000 that costs 3 cents per copy to operate. We can buy an IBM copying machine for only $800, but it costs 4 cents per copy to operate. At what level of activity (number of copies made) does one option offer a cost advantage over the other? Which machine should we start with and which machine should we switch to? The formula for this calculation is:

$$N = \frac{FC2 - FC1}{VC1 - VC2}$$

where

N = crossover point
$FC2$ = fixed cost of machine #2 (IBM; $ 800)
$FC1$ = fixed cost of machine #1 (Xerox; $1000)
$VC2$ = variable cost of machine #2 (IBM; $ .04)
$VC1$ = variable cost of machine #1 (Xerox; $ .03)

Putting the variables from our hypothetical situation into the formula, we get:

$$N = \frac{800 - 1000}{.03 - .04} = \frac{-200}{-.01} = 20{,}000 \text{ units}$$

N, the point of indifference, also known as the crossover point, is equal to the fixed cost (or purchase price) of machine 2 (FC_2) minus the fixed cost (or purchase price) of machine 1 (FC_1) divided by the variable cost (cost per copy) of machine 1 (VC_1) minus the variable cost (cost per copy) of machine 2 (VC_2). We can see that, if we were to make exactly 20,000 copies, it would make no difference which machine we would choose. In practice, the machine with lower fixed cost would generally be preferred for quantities below the crossover point. Double check: To find the machine that would be best for less than 20,000 units, we would compare the total cost of each machine at 19,999 units (1 unit less than the point of indifference) and at 20,001 (1 unit more than the point of indifference). We then find that the IBM machine is preferable for quantities up to the point of indifference, whereas the Xerox machine is preferable for quantities at or above the crossover point. The formulas for these calculations are:

$FC + VC \times$ (one unit below the point of indifference)

Xerox: $1000 + .03(19999) = \$1599.97$
IBM: $800 + .04(19999) = \$1599.96$

IBM is less expensive for less than 20,000 units.

$FC + VC \times$ (one unit above the point of indifference)

Xerox: $1000 + .03(20001) = \$1600.03$
IBM: $800 + .04(20001) = \$1600.04$

Xerox is less expensive for more than 20,000 units.

Crossover analysis has several major limitations. It does not factor the time value of money into calculations. Also, in practice, we may not be able to forecast the number of copies that we will need to make within a particular time frame. Moreover, it assumes that both options are equivalent in specifications. (This refers to such variables as copy quality, serviceability, and duration of warranty, and so on.)

BREAK-EVEN ANALYSIS

Break-even analysis allows us to determine the point at which we can expect to recoup an investment. The calculation for break-even can be based on (1) the quantity of units which must be produced/served, (2) total sales volume generated, or (3) selling price per unit (see Figure 3.7). Typically, costs exceed revenues (i.e., operating "in the red") at the outset of an undertaking, and this gap is narrowed until revenues meet costs (at the break-even point) and eventually exceed costs (i.e., operating "in the black").

Quantity

To find the break-even point based on the number of units that must be produced/served, we divide the fixed cost by the price minus the variable cost. The formula for this calculation is:

$$Bq = \frac{FC}{P - VC}$$

where

Bq = break-even quantity (the B/E point expressed in units)
FC = fixed cost, at $800
P = price, at $6 per unit
VC = variable cost, at $2 per unit

Putting the variables from our hypothetical situation into the formula, we get:

$$Bq = \frac{\$800}{\$6 - \$2} = 200 \text{ units}$$

Two hundred units would have to be sold to break-even.

Sales Volume

To find the break-even point based on sales volume, we add the fixed cost to the variable cost multiplied by the number of units. The formula for this calculation is:

$$Bsv = FC + VC(Q)$$

FIGURE 3.7 CHARTING THE BREAK-EVEN POINT

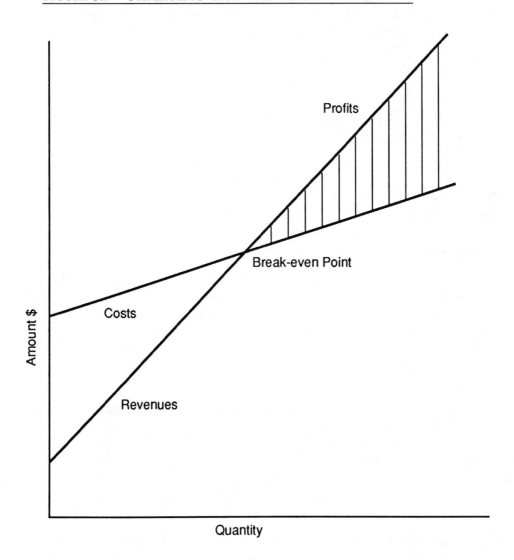

where

Bsv = break-even sales volume (the break-even point expressed
      in sales revenues)
FC = fixed cost, at $800
VC = variable cost, at $10
Q   = quantity, at 200 units

Putting the variables from our hypothetical situation into the formula, we get:

$$Bsv = \$800 + \$10(200) = \$2,800$$

The $2,800 in sales revenues would have to be generated in order to break-even.

Unit Price

To find the break-even point based on selling price, we add the fixed cost to the variable cost multiplied by the number of units and then divide this sum by the number of units. The formula for this calculation is:

$$Bp = \frac{FC + VC(Q)}{Q}$$

where

Bp = break-even price (the B/E point expressed as the selling price)
FC = fixed cost, at $800
VC = variable cost, at $10
Q   = quantity, at 200 units

$$Bp = \frac{\$800 + \$10(200)}{200} = \$14$$

A price of $14 per unit would have to be charged to break even.

The major limitation to break-even analysis is that it doesn't factor in the time value of money. (As with the payback method, this may not be a significant issue if time horizons for recoupment of investments are relatively short.)

LINEAR PROGRAMMING

LP allows us to determine the optimal mix of competing options in an investment or production environment, to increase profits in the face of financial and/or physical constraints (see capital rationing in Chapter 2 on accounting and finance). If, for example, we are in the construction/ real estate business building tennis courts and golf courses, we would like to know how many of each to invest in. Or, as in the example that follows (Figure 3.8), we are musical instrument manufacturers who produce only guitars and pianos.

Note: In "real life," it would be difficult to calculate the solution for a situation involving more than two "unknowns" without the use of a computer. Therefore, the following hypothetical case has been simplified for illustrative purposes so that the production of musical instruments involves only two tasks or steps in the production process. In actuality, production involves many more tasks. With a computer, solution would be very simple. LP computation is virtually always done by machine.

It takes 2 hours to assemble each guitar and 1 hour to paint it, while it takes 1 hour to assemble each piano and 3 hours to paint it. We have only 1,000 hours to assemble guitars and/or pianos, and only 1,200 hours to paint guitars and/or pianos. We anticipate that we will make a profit of $200 on each guitar and $300 on each piano. So our linear programming questions are:

How many guitars should we make?

How many pianos should we make?

How much profit will we make?

To find the answers to these questions, we translate the aforementioned "givens" [(A), (B), and (C)] into the simple algebraic language that you learned in high school [(a), (b), and (c)]. We find for one unknown P (for piano) by taking equation $2G + 1P \le 1,000$ (A) and moving $2G$ to the other side of the equal sign so that $1P \le 1,000 - 2G$ (a). P is equal to or less than $(1,000 - 2G)$, and we substitute $(1,000 - 2G)$ (b) for P on the second line of "algebraic computations," which corresponds to (B). We find that since G and P represent the optimal number of guitars and pianos to make within the limits of production capacity, we should make 360 guitars and 280 pianos. When we multiply these figures by the projected profit for

---

FIGURE 3.8   LINEAR PROGRAMMING

Given:

[Tasks]	Guitar	Piano	Capacity
(A) Assembling	2 hours per unit	1 hr per unit	1,000 hours
(B) Painting	1 hour per unit	3 hrs per unit	1,200 hours

(C) Unit profit: $200 + $300

(c) Objective function: $200G + $300P$ = profit

Questions:

How many guitars and pianos should we manufacture?
How much profit should we make?

(A) Constraints: $2G + 1P \leq 1,000$
(B) $1G + 3P \leq 1,200$

Algebraic computations:
   $1P \leq 1,000 - 2G$
   $1G + 3 (1,000 - 2G) \leq 1,200$
   $1G + 3,000 - 6G \leq 1,200$
   $-5G = -1,800$
   $G = 360$
   $2(360) + 1P \leq 1,000$
   $720 + P \leq 1,000$
   $P = 280$

Answers:

Manufacture 360 guitars and 280 pianos.
Anticipate $72,000 profit on guitars and $84,000 profit on pianos.

guitars ($200 times G) and for pianos ($300 times P), we find that we can anticipate receiving $72,000 and $84,000, respectively.

Although LP is a very valuable tool, it does carry with it a major limitation: not all situations can be viewed as linear. (Sophisticated computer programs can adjust for this, if they include a so-called "step" component.) Nonlinearity can reflect, for example, a bottleneck in production due to physical breakdown or work stoppage. Moreover, the projected unit profit would have to change as a result of changes in wages (e.g., overtime) or other costs (e.g., quantity discounts).

NETWORK ANALYSIS

Network analysis helps us to forecast the points of completion for projects we may choose to undertake. It provides analytical frameworks or formulas that can be used to transform subjective or "soft" information (or opinions) into somewhat more tangible projections or "solutions" to planning problems. Critical path and PERT are the most popular of the network analysis methods. *Critical Path* allows us to identify junctures at which delays are likely to occur. *PERT (project evaluation and review technique)* enables us to factor in optimistic and pessimistic (i.e., early and late) projections of project completion time.

Critical Path

This method depicts a series of linked or critical paths that lead to project completion. The critical path is the longest path of them all and represents the amount of time necessary to complete the project. The technique was originally introduced at E. I. du Pont de Nemours.

Figure 3.9 represents the critical path involved in building a scientific research center. Tasks A through F must be successfully accomplished to complete the project. In addition, certain steps must be completed before others can be started. We refer to these as "predecessor" steps. In situations where tasks overlap (as with tasks B and C), we count only the longer/longest of these tasks, since counting more than one could have the effect of overstating the time necessary to complete the project. We may be able to accelerate completion by enhancing overlapping of tasks.

FIGURE 3.9   IDENTIFYING THE CRITICAL PATH FOR BUILDING A RESEARCH CENTER

Given:

Tasks		Time	Predecessor
A	Forecast demand	2 months	—
B	Design facilities	5 months	A
C	Select equipment	4 months	A
D	Construction	7 months	B
E	Installation	3 months	C, D
F	Fine-tuning	1 month	E

Question:

How long will it take to complete this project?

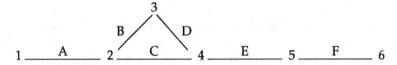

Answer:

It will take 18 months.
But if tasks A, B, and C can be performed
simultaneously . . .

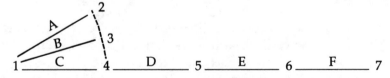

Answer:

It will take only 16 months.

Project Evaluation and Review Technique (PERT)

PERT was first used by the military in development of the Polaris submarine. The method exists in two forms. As a deterministic technique (i.e., one in which all activity times are assumed to be known with certainty), it is virtually indistinguishable from the critical path method "and the differences, if any, are only historical."[19] However, as a stochastic technique (i.e., one in which all activity times are assumed to be random variables), project managers are called upon to assign three subjective time estimates for each component or task. The optimistic estimate (i.e., early) is multiplied by 1, realistic by 4, and pessimistic by 1. These three weighted estimates are added together and then divided by 6. The formula for this calculation is:

$$Tc = \frac{a + 4b + c}{6}$$

where

Tc = time of completion for each task
a = optimistic estimate
b = realistic estimate
c = pessimistic estimate

Referring to the example provided for critical path and using totally arbitrary numbers to illustrate an application (see Figure 3.10), we can use this formula to calculate the time of completion for each task. By adding the values of each of the tasks comprising the critical path (note that path C is not a part of the critical path), we can obtain an estimate of how long the project will take.

THE PARETO PRINCIPLE: 80/20 RULE

The noted economist Vilfredo Pareto was an avid amateur gardener. In active pursuit of his avocation, he observed that roughly 20 percent of the peapods in his garden yielded 80 percent of the peas that could be harvested. As abstracted and applied to human resources management and operations management in the context of quality (TQM), the *80/20 rule*

FIGURE 3.10   PERT CALCULATIONS FOR ESTIMATION OF PROJECT COMPLETION TIME

Given:

Task	Optimistic	Realistic	Pessimistic
A Forecast demand	1 month	2 months	4 months
B Design facilities	3 months	5 months	6 months
C Select equipment	2 months	4 months	5 months
D Construction	5 months	7 months	9 months
E Installation	1 month	3 months	4 months
F Fine-tuning	$1/2$ month	1 month	$2^1/_2$ months

$$A \quad \frac{1 + 4(2) + 4}{6} \quad = \quad \frac{13}{6} = 2^1/_6$$

$$B \quad \frac{3 + 4(5) + 6}{6} \quad = \quad \frac{29}{6} = 4^5/_6$$

$$C \quad \frac{2 + 4(4) + 5}{6} \quad = \quad \left(\frac{23}{6} = 3^5/_6\right): \text{not counted}$$

$$D \quad \frac{5 + 4(7) + 9}{6} \quad = \quad \frac{42}{6} = 7$$

$$E \quad \frac{1 + 4(3) + 4}{6} \quad = \quad \frac{17}{6} = 2^5/_6$$

$$F \quad \frac{1/2 + 4(1) + 1^1/_2}{6} \quad = \quad \frac{6}{6} = \frac{1}{17^5/_6 \text{ months}}$$

If we sum the subtotals for tasks A, B, D, E, and F, we find that the project is likely to take $17^5/_6$ months to complete.

---

suggests, for example, that relatively few errors (i.e., input) can typically cause the lion's share of defects (i.e., output). (80/20 is also widely used by marketers to illustrate, for example, that relatively few of a company's salespeople may account for the majority of its sales volume or that relatively few of the brands in a company's product line may account for the majority of the firm's profits.)

QUEUING THEORY

This concept allows us to minimize the amount of time that customers (i.e., anyone we serve) must spend waiting (on line or in a queue) before they are served. Bank managers use queuing models to deploy human resources (i.e., tellers) efficiently, to minimize the time that customers must wait to be served. Facilities managers also program the computers that control multiple-elevator systems in large buildings so that the average time spent waiting for an elevator can be anticipated and minimized.

There is no single queuing formula. However, each is based upon prior experience. In other words, they consider the number of customers that can be expected to wait on line or be served at a given point in time, along with the likelihood that the size of the queue will substantially exceed the ability to accommodate customers in a timely manner. While the reduction of waiting time may incur increased costs, this must be weighed against the potential loss of customers resulting from poor service.

The Walt Disney amusement parks (such as Disneyland) are considered to be among the best-run facilities in terms of queuing considerations. While Disney's operations engineers are secretive about the methods they employ, some basic rules of queue management are commonly accepted:

- Establish a standard for maximum waiting time. (Disney's is 15 minutes.)
- "Distract" those who are waiting. Disney management knows that waiting time doesn't seem as long to customers if they are being entertained while waiting. (I recently visited an extremely popular restaurant for brunch. About ten parties were waiting to be seated before my guests and me, suggesting a wait of more than 15 minutes. Management astutely dispatched hostesses into the queue to serve complimentary coffee.)
- Conceal the queue. If potential customers can observe the line, they may be put off by it and decide not to wait on line at all. The better facilities are physically designed to "camouflage" or deflect attention from the queue.[20]

MONTE CARLO SIMULATION

The discussion of statistics in Chapter 4 underscores the importance of randomness in polling or testing. Toward that end, *Monte Carlo simulation* is a technique that has been widely employed to generate random numbers. (As you might imagine, the name is inspired by the gaming tables of Monaco.) It involves the use of mathematical formulas and is generally performed via computer. Given that randomness in sampling is linked to reliability of test results, applications of Monte Carlo abound in science, military strategy, and many other areas of endeavor, including business planning (e.g., forecasting prices and such). Employed to help forecast the probability of an event's occurrence, Monte Carlo has been particularly popular with production quality specialists as a means of identifying the point in time that a machine is likely to break down. For example, I am told that the U.S. Postal Service (USPS) uses similar statistical methods to forecast when parts in its optical character readers and other types of equipment are likely to fail. Having established a *predictive maintenance* program, the USPS is able to replace the parts shortly before they fail, thus averting processing stoppages. (Note: Critics of Monte Carlo simulation assert that the approach often generates nonrandom sets of numbers. Although such nonrandomness may be very subtle or "slight," it could be enough to cause an erroneous result.)[21]

JUST-IN-TIME PRODUCTION SYSTEM (JIT)

Developed by Taiichi Ohno of Toyota, inventory used in production is delivered to assembly lines just in time to avoid a stoppage in production. The benefits associated with this approach include enhancement of cash flow (as a result of reductions in inventory levels) and quality control (as a result of identification and correction of defects prior to or early in the production process).[22] Application to the food processing industry would seem particularly appropriate, in light of perishable inventory.

However, other fields have employed JIT with considerable success. For example, the Benetton clothing chain purportedly employs a variant of JIT. The firm manufactures sweaters without immediately dyeing them until orders indicate color preferences, at which point it dyes the items to meet demand.

Some critics of JIT, while appreciating the theoretical benefits of the approach, contend that in practice the process requires that inventory be ordered more frequently and in smaller quantities. (This suggests that economies of scale are not likely to be enjoyed.) So, they argue, the approach not only incurs additional ordering and carrying charges (i.e., costs), but is ultimately a rather cumbersome system, since it requires more labor, as well.

Moreover, the consequences of underestimating customer demand (and the corresponding required inventory) may call for managers to employ a *just-in-case* (JIC) approach, one that provides for a "cushion" or overage to accommodate additional demand.

ECONOMIC ORDER QUANTITY (EOQ) AND REORDER POINT (ROP)

These formulas were designed to help us determine the most *cost-effective size of an order* (EOQ) for merchandise and the *point in time at which we should reorder* (ROP), respectively. In practice, however, both formulas are greatly limited in their application since they are based upon the premise that we can forecast demand and lead time with precision, which we unfortunately cannot do.[23] (As you might imagine, EOQ and ROP are not congruent with JIT).

Clearly, our examination of JIT, EOQ, and ROP underscores the keystone importance of economies of scale as a business issue. These approaches share in common their association with costs of one type or another. JIT may incur purchasing inefficiencies in the interest of product/service quality, whereas EOQ and ROP may incur quality deficiencies in the interest of purchasing efficiencies.

THE HUMAN RESOURCES MANAGEMENT CHECKLIST

1. Do I motivate my subordinates based upon their needs as individuals as well as my needs as their manager?

2. What motivates me?

3. Can I be more sensitive to the personality characteristics of my subordinates? Can I deploy my staff more effectively as a result?

4. How does my personality relate to my strengths and weaknesses as a manager?

5. Should I use an MBO program or something like it to plan and evaluate performance?

6. How can I improve my communication skills?

7. What can I do to embrace total quality management (TQM)?

THE OPERATIONS MANAGEMENT CHECKLIST

1. Have I done all that I can to enhance economies of scale? Why might I deliberately *not* want to do so?

2. Can I readily calculate the break-even points of my projects?

3. Do I know when to switch from one machine to another in the interest of cost-effectiveness?

4. Am I making optimal use of my production and processing facilities?

5. Can I forecast completion dates of projects more accurately?

6. Can I minimize waiting time for internal as well as external customers?

7. Can I reduce inventory while improving quality standards?

RECOMMENDED READING

Boone, Lewis E., *Principles of Management* (New York: Random House, 1984).

Bolman, Lee G., and Terrence Deal, *Modern Approaches to Understanding and Managing Organizations* (San Francisco: Jossey-Bass, 1984).

Brabb, George J., *Introduction to Quantitative Management* (Homewood, IL: Richard D. Irwin, 1980).

Carlisle, Howard M., *Management Essentials* (New York: Science Research Associates, 1982).

Cook, Thomas M., *Contemporary Operations Management* (Englewood Cliffs, NJ: Prentice Hall, 1980).

Drucker, Peter F., *An Introductory View of Management* (New York: Harper's College Press, 1977).

ORGANIZATIONS AND RESOURCES

Academy of Management
P.O. Box 39
Ada, OH 45810
(419) 772-1953

American Management Association
135 W. 50th Street
New York, NY 10020
(212) 586-8100

American Society for Training and Development
Box 1443, 1630 Duke Street
Alexandria, VA 22313
(703) 683-8100

National Society for Performance and Instruction
1126 16th Street, N.W., Suite 102
Washington, D.C. 20036
(202) 861-0777

Operations Management Education and Research Foundation
P.O. Box 835991
Richardson, TX 75085
(214) 368-5393

Operations Research Society of America
Mt. Royal and Guilford Avenues
Baltimore, MD 21202
(301) 528-4146

Society for Human Resources Management
606 N. Washington Street
Alexandria, VA 22314
(703) 548-3440

ENDNOTES

1. Lee G. Bolman and Terrence Deal, *Modern Approaches to Understanding and Managing Organizations* (San Francisco: Jossey-Bass, 1984).

2. Abraham Maslow, *Motivation and Personality*, 2nd ed. (New York: Harper & Row, 1970).

3. J. F. Evered, *Shirt-Sleeves Management* (New York: AMACOM, 1981).

4. Douglas McGregor, *The Human Side of Enterprise* (New York: McGraw-Hill, 1960).

5. Bolman and Deal, *Modern Approaches to Understanding and Managing Organizations*.

6. Jean M. Kummerow, *Verifying Your Type Preferences* (Gainesville, FL: Center for Applications of Psychological Type, 1992).

7. Bolman and Deal, *Modern Approaches to Understanding and Managing Organizations* (San Francisco: Jossey-Bass, 1986).

8. W. Edwards Deming, *Quality, Productivity, and Competitive Position* (Cambridge, MA: Massachusetts Institute of Technology, 1982).

9. Philip Crosby, *Let's Talk Quality* (New York: McGraw-Hill, 1989).

10. Joseph M. Juran, *Juran's Quality Control Handbook*, 4th ed. (New York: McGraw-Hill, 1988)

11. William Ouchi, *Theory Z* (Reading, MA: Addison-Wesley, 1981).

12. Tom Peters, *Liberation Management* (New York: Alfred A. Knopf, 1992).

13. E. Hunninger, *The Arthur Young Manager's Handbook* (New York: Crown, 1986).

14. Ibid.

15. Milo Sobel, *The Secrets of Professionalism* (New York: The Coronet Consulting Group, 1986).

16. Ibid.

17. Leonard Nadler, *Designing Training Programs* (Reading, MA: Addison-Wesley, 1982).

18. Compiled by Elizabeth A. McDaniel, Assistant Vice President and Professor for Academic Affairs and Professor of Special Education, University of Hartford. Most of these suggestions are excerpted and paraphrased from a book by Raymond J. Wlodkowski, *Enhancing Adult Motivation to Learn*, published by Jossey-Bass, 1985.

19. Hamdy A. Taha, *Operations Research* (New York: Macmillan, 1976).

20. Richard Saltus, "Waiting—Scientists Have a Name for It: Queue Management," *Orange County Register*, November 1, 1992.

21. Malcolm W. Browne, "Coin-Tossing Computers Found to Show Subtle Bias," *The New York Times*, January 12, 1993.

22. Shigeo Shingo, *A Study of the Toyota Production System* (Cambridge, MA: Productivity Press, 1989).

23. Christine Ammer and Dean S. Ammer, *Dictionary of Business and Economics* (New York: The Free Press, 1984).

CHAPTER 4

STATISTICS

Statistics involves the gathering, organization, and mathematical analysis of information. Statistical methods enable business decision makers to characterize a given entity/population quantitatively, compare it to another or others, and arrive at meaningful insights. This latter process is commonly known as *statistical inference,* since we are often able to deduce or infer certain conclusions on the basis of statistical "evidence."

Applications of statistics can be very creative, well outside the realms of commerce and natural science. In the humanities, scholars have used statistical methods in their attempts to support or refute the contention that the works of William Shakespeare were in fact ghost written by his contemporary Francis Bacon. In sports, statistical methods can play an integral role in planning strategies and tactics on the playing field (i.e., coaching) as well as off (i.e., wagering).

In today's sophisticated business environment, virtually all types of statistically relevant data can be readily and easily retrieved and analyzed through the use of computers and a wide variety of programs generally available at computer software dealers. The user does not have to "crunch" numbers and plot out elaborate formulas. Instead, he or she need only to "plug in" raw numbers and program the process. In other words, don't sweat the calculations. Nevertheless, the decision maker should have a sufficient conceptual understanding of statistics to know which process (i.e., formula) to program, given its strengths and limitations.

When I studied statistics as a requisite part of my MBA curriculum, I really hated it . . . and now I realize why. Statistics, as typically taught in business schools, does not necessarily address "real-world" business concerns. Students learn formulas and punch these out on hand-held calculators, in the hope of arriving at "correct" answers on exams and assignments. They don't, however, learn to play "detective" and use statistics to address practical, everyday situations. Nor, for that matter, do they learn to anticipate the "political" nuances relating to the presentation of statistical information. After all, one may elect to present a glass as half empty or half full. In this regard, we will be sensitized to the notion that information can be organized and presented by us to further our cause best or organized and presented by others to our detriment. You will learn the distinction in this chapter.

CONDUCTING A RESEARCH PROJECT

How do managers obtain the information necessary to make optimal decisions? Welcome to the wonderful world of research! Areas of application include:

- Forecasting revenues
- Gauging competitive threats
- Examining consumer attitudes
- Evaluating advertising effectiveness
- Establishing pricing policy
- Gauging quality control

The information that management decision makers seek comes from a variety of sources and may be categorized as either primary research or secondary research. *Secondary research* is generally more readily available and less expensive. It is preexisting and can often be obtained from the following sources:

- Market research firms
- Advertising agencies
- Sales promotion firms
- Public relations firms
- Trade associations
- Professional associations
- Governmental agencies
- Quasi-governmental agencies
- Professional journals and publications
- Trade journals and publications
- Newspaper research departments
- Magazine research departments
- Mailing list firms
- Academic institutions

Primary research is not as yet created and must be made to order, so to speak. It can often be commissioned and obtained from a number of the aforementioned sources, or you can conduct your own market research project.

Steps in a Research Project

1. Define the problem.

   a. State the questions that are begging for answers.

   b. Be as specific as possible.

   c. Try not to accomplish too much at one time.

2. Formulate a plan and choose from among the following research methods.

   a. *Questionnaire Survey.* The question-and-answer approach—open or closed end or a combination—may be used as follows:

   Q: Do you own a VCR?

   A: Yes (or No).

Q: If "Yes," what brand?

A: Brand X.

Q: Why did you choose that brand?

A: Because . . .

b. *Observation.* This method—watching subjects using the product—is used with great success in the toy industry. (Researchers know that kids can find the most unusual ways of playing with toys, developing ingenious new applications . . . or unsafe ones.) Generally, however, ethical and legal issues may arise involving observation without informed consent.

c. *Experimentation.* Changing one variable (such as price) while keeping the others constant may be used in a market test situation prior to formal launch of the product and its broader distribution.

d. *Focus Group.* Group discussion involving current or potential users or customers requires a skilled moderator to "probe" effectively yet not in an obvious manner. For example, a major household appliance manufacturer conducted focus groups to determine how they might modify its product line to best satisfy housewives. Findings suggested that housewives wished that they had more surface area on the countertops. So the manufacturer decided to mount the entire new line of appliances under the kitchen cabinets.

3. Collect data via

a. *Telephone.* Immediate on-line entry of responses into data bases can be facilitated. Interviewer may "probe" beyond initial answers for "richer" information, but this method can be expensive.

b. *Mail.* Callers can reach a highly targeted survey sample, but response rates may be low. (In this single instance, "response" means participation.) Moreover, this method lacks interactivity and does not permit "probing" for additional information.

c. *In Person.* The human element enhances the opportunity to obtain "rich" information. However, interviewer cheating may occur. (Low-paid students who are often hired to conduct interviews in the field may falsify or distort interviews to complete more interviews on a piecework compensation basis.)

4. Analyze data. The raw information is organized and examined. Quantitative methods may be employed, especially in terms of probability and the relatedness of variables, or findings may be expressed more simply. For example, "nine out of ten respondents said they preferred our experimental new brand to Brand X."

5. State conclusions and make recommendations. Based upon the findings arising from analysis, marketing implications will emerge. For example, since nine out of ten respondents preferred the brand we are testing, we may decide to launch it on a national basis.

BASIC TERMINOLOGY

Populations, Samples, Randomness, Bias, and Representativeness

Political polls are a kind of study that we are all familiar with. It is impractical, if not actually impossible, to ask all voting members of a *population* or entire group in which we are interested (i.e., the total universe) what candidate they intend to vote for. Therefore, the poll taker must choose a *sample* or small percentage of the population on a *random basis*, so that *bias* is unlikely to distort the result of the study. In other words, the sample should, in microcosm, be *representative* of the entire voting population. A classic example of a study that failed to achieve this was the poll for the 1948 presidential election. Apparently, pollsters chose and relied upon a sample that was *unrepresentative* and biased in favor of Dewey, who ultimately lost to Truman.

Validity and Reliability

Obviously, a test must be able to measure accurately whatever it is designed to measure (*validity*) and to do so repeatedly (*reliability*).

Sometimes, tests are both invalid and unreliable. More dangerous, though, are tests that are invalid and reliable. It has been argued, for example, that exam questions dealing with sports points of reference can reflect a bias against females (who tend to find these points of reference unfamiliar due to cultural norms).

The various statistical tests outlined in this chapter help us to analyze data and to infer certain conclusions about the subject of our research. These tests yield numerical values (e.g., t values for t-test; F for analysis of variance) and are listed in statistical tables, similar to the way mortgage payment schedules are listed in financial tables. When these values fall within certain parameters, we may be able to draw conclusions from the data. For example, we might find that the relationships being tested are very strong or "significant" and that they (in a sense) "validate" our hypothesis, the assumption or "hunch" that we are testing.

But to what extent is the test result "reliable"? In other words, we want to know what the margin of error or confidence interval is. This is often expressed as a p or *probability value*. P values usually appear in any of three forms:

$P \leq .01$ indicates that the findings are likely to occur at least 99 percent of the time and that the margin of error is not likely to be greater than 1 percent

$P \leq .05$ indicates that the findings are likely to occur at least 95 percent of the time and that the margin of error is not likely to be greater than 5 percent

$P \leq .10$ indicates that the findings are likely to occur at least 90 percent of the time and that the margin of error is not likely to be greater than 10 percent

The selection of a confidence interval should be appropriate to the circumstances at hand. For example, the standard for conducting an exploratory study might be less stringent than the standard for a more critical or definitive follow-up project. So it might be more practical to use .05 than .01. (If we want to increase the confidence level, that is, decrease the margin of error, we would use a larger sample. However, this might prove to be more expensive or require more time.) If, on the other hand, you are reviewing a vendor's specifications regarding the integrity or performance of his product, you might require a probability value of .01 rather than .05 in your capacity as a discriminating customer.

Frequency Distributions

In analyzing the information we gather, we would certainly be interested in the degree to which the *observations* (i.e., the people polled in the survey) are clustered or dispersed, similar or different. The degree of variation in the data is commonly referred to as dispersion. This characteristic may be depicted graphically and is known as a distribution.

Distributions generally take on any of three forms:

Symmetrical

This type takes on the shape of a normal or bell curve, with most observations appearing at the midrange and other observations falling equally on both sides. (See Figure 4.1.) Clothing manufacturers, for example, go with a production run that yields a relatively small proportion of very small as well as very large sizes, a larger proportion of somewhat small as well as somewhat large sizes, and the greatest proportion of sizes in the range of what is "average" (and we will define and calculate "average" very shortly).

FIGURE 4.1   SYMMETRICAL DISTRIBUTION

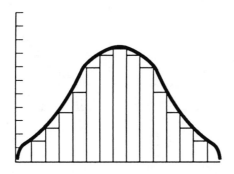

Skewed

This type takes on the shape of a curve that "favors" a certain range of values over others. (See Figure 4.2.) For example, the distribution in Figure 4.2(a) can be said to be skewed downward, and conversely, the distribution in Figure 4.2(b) can be said to be skewed upward. Given that the range of values represent income levels for each of two communities, ranked lowest to highest (left to right), and that the range is the same for both communities, we would conclude that the community represented by Figure 4.2 seems to be relatively impoverished, whereas the other seems to be relatively wealthy.

Bimodal

This type takes on the shape of two "Siamese" curves that have been joined together. (See Figure 4.3.) It represents a situation in which there are two "clusters" or many observations at each of two values. Figure 4.3 could represent that test grades for a particular class marked by a preponderance of grades that are "low" and "high," with considerably fewer grades that fall somewhere in between.

FIGURE 4.2   SKEWED DISTRIBUTION

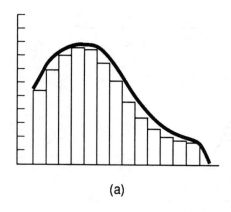

(a)

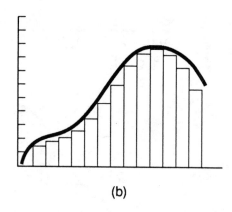

(b)

FIGURE 4.3   BIMODAL DISTRIBUTION

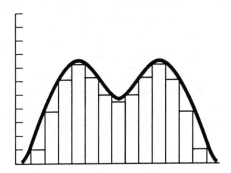

KEY STATISTICAL MEASURES

While distributions are useful in that they characterize how observations appear in the aggregate and can be depicted graphically, other measures allow us to quantify information and to organize it so that we can make better decisions. Such measures include the following:

Measures of Central Tendency

Mean

Mean is a fancy word for average. The way we figure out an average is to divide the total or sum of all observations by the total number of observations. Let's assume that there are 7 salespeople (or observations) in a sales department. The number of product units sold by these individuals in June is 1 + 9 + 10 + 12 + 13 + 17 + 17 + . . . , or 79, if you sum them. If we divide 79 by 7, we find that the average number of sales per salesperson in June is 11.28 units.

If we were sales managers, we might compare the mean number of sales for June with the means for previous months, to see if there is some kind of trend. An advantage to using the mean for this purpose rather than absolute sales volume measured in dollars is that it would allow us to examine the level of productivity of the sales force. Specifically, sales volume might increase merely because more people were hired to sell, not because they did a better job. So, if there were 14 salespeople employed next June (twice the number working this year, a 100 percent increase) and total sales dollars increased by 50 percent, productivity and profitability would have declined despite an increase in sales revenues.

Median

The *median* is the middle number in a series of numbers when ranked in value from low to high. We calculate the median by taking the number of observations +1 and then dividing that sum by 2. In the previous example, we have 7 salespeople. 7 + 1 (or 8) divided by 2 equals 4. The fourth number in the sequence is the median. In this instance, the median is 12.

$$1, 9, 10, [12], 13, 17, 17$$

The median tends to "screen out" extreme values. As we review the performance of our 7 salespeople, we notice that one of them turned in a performance considerably lower than all the others, selling only one single unit in June. A median would serve to "camouflage" this poor performance, as evidenced in this instance by a median of 12.0 compared to a mean of only 11.28. The sales manager who wishes to put his or her best foot forward, so to speak, would obviously prefer to use the median. If, however, the salesperson who sold only one unit was to have sold 35 units instead, the sales manager would prefer to include or even highlight this outstanding performance in his or her report, rather than deemphasize it. Therefore, the mean would be preferred.

Mode

The *mode* is simply the observation or number that appears most often. In this case, the number 17 happens to appear more often than any other number, so it is the mode.

$$1, 9, 10, 12, 13, [17], [17]$$

Identifying the mode can help you decide how to prioritize and where to concentrate your efforts. This can readily be applied to marketing, regarding the concentrated marketing strategy. To take best advantage of limited financial resources, for example, a manufacturer may decide to produce an initial production run in a single color. Given that this variable may be "coded" numerically (i.e., 1 = red, 9 = blue, 17 = green), the mode for the color variable would suggest the color of choice.

Measures of Dispersion

Range

Range simply describes how much of a "spread" there is between the highest and lowest numbers, the extreme values. Using the same values provided under "measures of central tendency," we find that the lowest number is 1 and the highest is 17. So we subtract 1 from 17, and we can easily see that the spread or range is 16. The range does not, however, describe where most of the observations or numbers are "clustered."

Standard Deviation

Standard deviation is a primary indicator of the extent to which our observations deviate from the mean. This measure is calculated by subtracting the mean from each observation, squaring the subtotals, adding them up, dividing them by the number of observations, and finally finding the square root.

The formula for standard deviation is:*

$$\sqrt{\frac{\Sigma(X - \bar{x})^2}{N}}$$

where

$\bar{x}$ = mean
X = actual value of each observation
N = number of observations

*This formula pertains to application wherein all observations of the entire population are included. If, however, standard deviation is used with a random sample, such that the observations in the sample are assumed to be representative of the population, the denominator of the formula should be "$N - 1$" rather than "N."

STANDARD DEVIATION, EXAMPLE 1   Using the sales department example described in the section on Mean, we have a series of 7 numbers to plug into the formula, as well as the mean itself.

	[X]	[x̄]	[X − x̄]²
Salesperson 1 sold	1 unit	1 − 11.28 =	10.28 squared = 105.68
2	9 units	9 − 11.28 =	2.28 squared = 5.20
3	10 units	10 − 11.28 =	1.28 squared = 1.64
4	12 units	12 − 11.28 =	0.72 squared = 0.52
5	13 units	13 − 11.28 =	1.72 squared = 2.96
6	17 units	17 − 11.28 =	5.72 squared = 32.72
7	17 units	17 − 11.28 =	5.72 squared = 32.72
N = 7			181.44

$$\sqrt{\frac{\Sigma(X - \bar{x})^2}{N}} = \sqrt{\frac{181.44}{7}} = \sqrt{25.92} = 5.09$$

The standard deviation is 5.09.

Nobody I know regularly figures out standard deviation without a computer or calculator. And to put your mind totally at rest, each and every quantitative formula in this book and, for that matter, in any university-based MBA course of study, is calculated by machine. You need only to punch in the raw numbers.

Central Limit Theorem

To appreciate the value of the standard deviation, we must first understand that it only makes sense within the context of what is known as the central limit theorem. For our immediate purposes, I ask that you accept on faith the following:

1. No matter what type of distribution you have (i.e., normal or otherwise), the mean of your sample will roughly approximate the mean of your entire population.

2. To be representative of the population, a sample size of at least 30 observations is required.

3. Of all observations (see Figure 4.4),

34 percent will fall within the 1st "section" ABOVE the mean

34 percent will fall within the 1st "section" BELOW the mean

13 percent will fall within the 2nd "section" ABOVE the mean

13 percent will fall within the 2nd "section" BELOW the mean

3 percent will fall within the 3rd "section" ABOVE the mean

3 percent will fall within the 3rd "section" BELOW the mean

4. "Section" is, for the moment, synonymous with standard deviation.

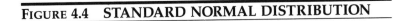

FIGURE 4.4   STANDARD NORMAL DISTRIBUTION

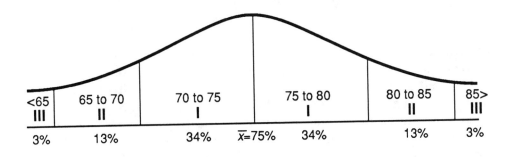

So, if you are the vice president of sales overseeing 100 salespeople and the mean annual sales is 75 units per salesperson and the standard deviation is 5 (rather than 5.09, to use a whole number for ease of math computation), you will find that:

34 (34%) of your salespeople sold between 75 and 80 units

34 (34%) of your salespeople sold between 70 and 75 units

13 (13%) of your salespeople sold between 80 and 85 units

13 (13%) of your salespeople sold between 65 and 70 units

3 (3%) of your salespeople sold more than 85 units

3 (3%) of your salespeople sold fewer than 65 units

Note that there is a range of 5 (the standard deviation) for each "section," except those at the extremes.

Since 94 salespeople (94 percent) fall within two standard deviations from the mean and sell more than 65 but less than 85 units, it may be said that there is not a great deal of dispersion, that there is not a great deal of variation in the data.

STANDARD DEVIATION, EXAMPLE 2   Standard deviation is a very important indicator for portfolio managers and other investment counselors. Assume that the financial advisor is weighing two investment options which are likely to yield a similar mean dividend, yet one has a low standard deviation while the other has a high standard deviation. Given that high standard deviation (i.e., in the form of wide swings or fluctuations) in this context is indicative of exposure to risk, a senior citizen client living on a fixed and ostensibly limited income would probably be discouraged from investing in the option with the high standard deviation. Securities analysts find it useful to use the beta factor to reflect the degree of a stock's volatility relative to the market in general. If beta is 1.25, this means that the stock is 25 percent more volatile than the market viewed as a whole. The lower the beta, the better.[1]

Note: The examples we have used for mean, median, and mode involve observations which comprise the entire population (i.e., 7 observations) rather than a mere sample of the population. Therefore, due to the purely descriptive nature of our sample, it is okay to use the standard deviation even though we have fewer than 30 observations. Aside from this exception, we might elect to use the standard error for samples of fewer than 30 observations.

A STATISTICAL ANECDOTE: WHAT IS "NORMAL"?

I'd like to share a personal anecdote with you to underscore further the practical applications of statistics.

I was concerned about hair loss from my scalp, so I recently visited my dermatologist. He asked approximately how many hairs I lose each day. Is it more than 25? My response was that I hadn't even thought of it in those terms, only in terms of perceived thinning. When pressed for an answer, I reluctantly suggested that it is possible. He then asked whether the figure is less than 100, to which I responded with somewhat greater confidence that it was. He then explained that this was "normal." Upon hearing this, I shared with him my sense of relief since I thought that I was going bald. My sense of well-being was instantly shattered by his comment, "Oh, you're going bald, but that's normal."

In retrospect, I find this episode sort of funny because the word "normal" meant something different to me than it did to my physician. To me, "normal" meant that "it's okay" or even "desirable." I viewed the term judgmentally, that bald is bad. To the dermatologist, "normal" meant nothing more than "common in occurrence." In statistical terms, he was saying that my mild case of male pattern (or genetically induced) baldness falls within one standard deviation of the mean, that some thinning of hair is very common among men in their late thirties. This was not a value judgment on his part, merely an objective observation.

STORIES BEHIND THE STATISTICS: CREATIVE INTERPRETATION

Scenario 1: Low Dispersion

Figure 4.5 depicts a symmetrical distribution with little dispersion. Let's assume that each of those little square boxes clustered near the mean represents the job evaluation of an employee in a given department

FIGURE 4.5 LOW-DISPERSION DISTRIBUTION SCENARIO

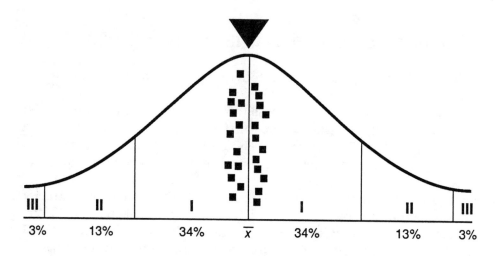

III	II	I	$\overline{x}$	I	II	III
3%	13%	34%		34%	13%	3%

of your company. Assume you are the personnel director and you routinely examine this diagram as an illustration of what's going on in this department. What do you suspect this distribution signifies? (Remember: Even the best of detectives have many suspects before they ultimately arrest the guilty culprit.)

One possibility is that everybody in the department is producing at about the same level. If they work on an assembly line, it might indicate a union-encouraged work slowdown or perhaps merely a highly collegial and noncompetitive working environment having nothing whatsoever to do with a union, in which no employee wants to show up or outperform his or her peers. Another possibility is that the manager of this department is an indiscriminate and poor evaluator.

Scenario 2: High Dispersion

Figure 4.6 depicts a bimodal distribution with considerable dispersion. Let's assume that you are routinely examining this diagram as an illustration of what's going on in another department. What do you suspect might be going on here? One possibility is that the evaluations are actually fair and accurate and, if so, that one grouping or segment of employees was poorly trained while the other segment was properly trained, or that one was not properly motivated and the other one was properly motivated. A more ominous possibility is that the manager of this department is a biased and unfair evaluator. This suspicion could be quickly supported or refuted by exploring further to see whether or not the grouping that has received the less favorable evaluations is comprised

FIGURE 4.6 HIGH-DISPERSION DISTRIBUTION SCENARIO

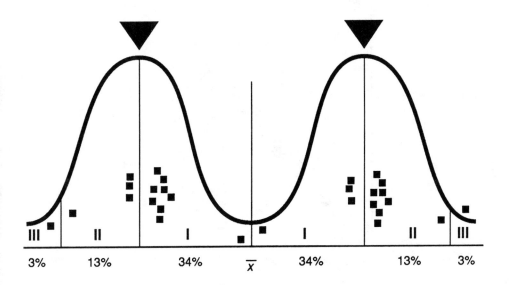

primarily of minorities such as people of color or women, while the grouping which has received the more favorable evaluations is comprised of middle-aged white males. Toward this end, you might want to examine *each* of the personnel files for this department and perhaps also interview a cross section of employees as well as the manager. (This scenario presumes, of course, that the manager of this department is white and perhaps male, as well.)

REGRESSION ANALYSIS

Regression analysis[2] is a statistical method that allows us to examine the relationship that exists between variables. It is commonly used in forecasting. It does not, however, suggest that one variable is caused by another, only that a relationship exists and that we can ascribe a magnitude of strength to the relationship. To quote Wallace Irwin, statistics show that of those who contract the habit of eating, very few survive.

**FIGURE 4.7   EXAMPLE OF POSITIVE CORRELATION
COEFFICIENT. *R* IS POSITIVE.**

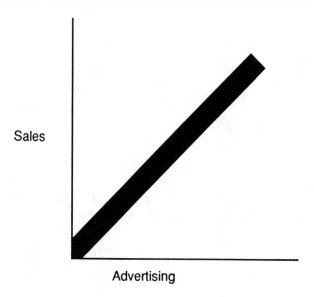

Sales

Advertising

The *correlation coefficient,* denoted by *r,* reflects the magnitude of the relationship. If the *r* value is close to +1, there is an extremely strong positive relationship. (With any value less than +1, we cannot.) Such is the case between the variables of sales and advertising in Figure 4.7. As advertising increases, sales increase, too. Conversely, if the *r* value is close to -1, there is a strong negative relationship. Such is the case between the variables of sales and interest rates (see Figure 4.8). As interest rates increase, sales decrease.

Regression analysis is almost always done by computer, requiring only that the raw numbers be inputted. The software does the rest. If you wanted to find the *r* value manually, it would be a time-consuming process.

The *coefficient of determination,* denoted by r^2 (i.e., the *r* value squared), reflects the degree to which other variables are related. If we arbitrarily assume that $r^2 = .25$, we can then say that only 25 percent of the variation in sales is related to the variation in interest rates (or advertising expenditures).

FIGURE 4.8   EXAMPLE OF NEGATIVE CORRELATION COEFFICIENT. *R* IS NEGATIVE.

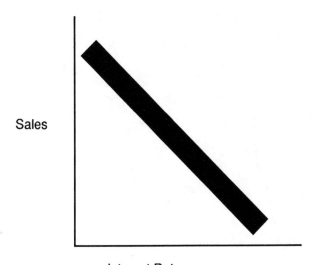

Sales

Interest Rates

TIME SERIES ANALYSIS

Time series analysis[3] allows us to observe performance of a given behavior or variable over a period of time. Like regression analysis, it is commonly employed in forecasting and involves plotting a line. We refer to this as a trend line, and it appears with three other lines representing variations (see Figure 4.9) as follows:

1. Secular trend (general trend)
2. Seasonal variation (periodic or regular phenomenon)
3. Cyclical variation (economic cycle, one year plus)
4. Irregular variation (random or chance events)

   Trend analysis can be more simple and primitive, of course. A single-line representation can easily be created by, for example, posting sales

FIGURE 4.9   TIME SERIES ANALYSIS

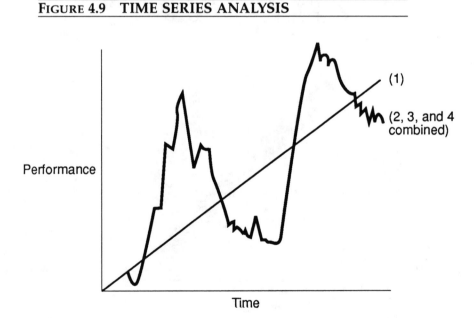

figures for each month in a one- or two-year time frame and connecting the dots to form a line.

There are other statistical methods that you are unlikely to use on a regular, "hands-on" basis. It is not necessary that you know how to perform these tests. However, you should understand that statistical tables can help you determine whether or not values or results yielded by the tests are significant and to what extent you can rely on them.

OTHER PARAMETRIC STATISTICAL METHODS

The following methods[4] also require normal distributions, those with observations of 30 or more. However, the vast majority of managers and decision makers, unless they are in highly technical areas, such as research or engineering, are not likely to be using these:

The *t-test* (expressed as a *t* value) allows us to examine the means of two discrete groups and to compare the groups regarding some variable (e.g., gender).

Analysis of Variance or *ANOVA* (expressed as an *F* value) is similar to the t-test, but it allows us to compare more than two groups or variables (e.g., gender, ethnicity, age).

NONPARAMETRIC STATISTICAL METHODS[5]

The following statistical tests do not require normal distributions:

Chi Square Analysis

χ^2 allows us to examine a limited set of values (e.g., male or female) to help determine if a variable is related to behavior or a state of nature (e.g., gender re attendance).

Poisson Distribution

λ allows us to estimate the probability of an occurrence (e.g., that a production line will suffer a bottleneck).

A REMINDER . . .

Although there are additional statistical methods explained in other text-books, the aforementioned ones represent those commonly used by management decision makers. Please keep in mind that these are generally calculated by computer and that software is widely available to allow inputting of raw numbers, yielding desired "answers" or information. In other words, you don't have to know the formulas.

THE STATISTICS CHECKLIST

1. Have I used the best research methods to serve my purpose and budget?
2. Have I gathered the necessary information randomly and without bias?
3. Do the tests or methods that are used yield valid and reliable results?
4. What do measures of central tendency and dispersion reveal about what I am studying?

RECOMMENDED READING

Adler, Irving, *Probability and Statistics for Everyman* (New York: John Day, 1963).

Averill, E. W., *Elements of Statistics* (New York: John Wiley and Sons, 1972).

Berenson, Mark L., *Basic Business Statistics* (Englewood Cliffs, NJ: Prentice Hall, 1983).

Parket, I. Robert, *Statistics for Business Decision Making* (New York: Random House, 1974).

ORGANIZATIONS AND RESOURCES

American Statistics Association
1429 Duke Street
Alexandria, VA 22314
(703) 684-1221

ENDNOTES

1. Christine Ammer and Dean S. Ammer, *Dictionary of Business and Economics* (New York: The Free Press, 1984).

2. I. Robert Parket, personal correspondence, 1993.

3. I. Robert Parket, *Statistics for Business Decision Making* (New York: Random House, 1974).

4. George J. Brabb, *Introduction to Quantitative Management* (New York: Holt, Rinehart and Winston, 1968).

5. Hamdy A. Taha, *Operations Research: An Introduction* (New York: Macmillan, 1976).

CHAPTER 5

ECONOMICS

Economics is widely regarded as the theoretical sister of finance, which, in contrast, may be regarded as a more practical discipline. To support this contention, George Bernard Shaw once said, "If all economists in the world were laid end to end, they still wouldn't reach a conclusion." Economics is occasionally referred to as "the dismal science." This is attributed to the pessimistic influence of Thomas Malthus (1766–1834), who prognosticated dire consequences as the result of population increasing geometrically while the means of subsistence increase only arithmetically.

Economics involves the study of human behavior as it relates to the consumption and utilization of resources to satisfy wants. The social sciences are often drawn upon, since so much of economic behavior and decision making is influenced by motives and incentives. Economics is also concerned with methods of organizing the production, distribution, and sharing of goods and services. In fact, the word is derived from two Greek words, *oikos*, "house," and *nemein*, "to manage." Apparently, the principles gleaned from the management of households may also be employed for substantially larger units, such as businesses, cities, countries, and groups of countries. *Macroeconomics* is the branch of economics that deals with analysis of broad and general aspects of an economy. In contrast, *microeconomics* is the branch of economics that deals with analysis of particular aspects of an economy.

MACROECONOMICS

Primary macroeconomic concerns include assessment of:

Aggregate income (as reflected by gross national product and gross domestic product)

Employment (as reflected by unemployment level)

Price (as reflected by the Consumer Price Index and the Producer Price Index)

GNP and GDP

Aggregate income is measured by *gross national product (GNP)*, the total amount of goods and services produced *by* a nation or by *gross domestic product (GDP)*, the total amount of goods and services produced *within* a nation. The latter indicator has taken on increasingly greater significance in light of the trend of American businesses to produce outside the nation's borders, with the intent of substantially reducing labor and other costs.

GNP and GDP each consist of consumer spending (i.e., individual/general public buying), investment spending (i.e., commercial buying), and government spending. Both indicators should be viewed in light of a positive net trade balance, such that exports exceed imports. The formula for GNP or GDP is:

$$\text{GNP or GDP} = C + I + G$$

where

C = consumer spending
I = investment spending
G = government spending

Consider, if you will, the following: approximately 12 percent of American GNP is generated by the medical and health care segments of the economy. Is this good or bad? Well, one view suggests that it is a good thing that a nation can afford to devote such a large slice of the pie to the health of its people, whereas a divergent position suggests that it should be a matter of great concern that the nation's people are so unhealthy as to require so much in the way of care. Moreover, medical and health care (and services, generally speaking) are not universally regarded as truly "productive" in the sense that the manufacture and delivery of tangible goods are. What do you think?

Employment

Actually, unemployment. The distinction is drawn between frictional, structural, and cyclical unemployment. *Frictional* refers to individuals who are out of work for relatively short periods of time due to such varied reasons as pregnancies and career transitions, as well as seasonal dislocations. *Structural* refers to individuals who are out of work for extended periods of time due to a lack of skills, such as the "hard-core" unemployed of the inner cities and those whose considerable skills have been rendered obsolete by automation and new technologies. "Full" employment suggests that the structural component is very low and that the frictional component is at a "normal" level. *Cyclical* refers to individuals who are out of work due to downturns in economic cycles.

Price

Changes in price are measured by the *Consumer Price Index (CPI)*, the indicator of choice for retail prices of goods and services, and the *Producer Price Index (PPI)*, the indicator of choice for wholesale prices of goods and not services at the manufacturer's door. These measures compare price levels against those associated with a base year. So, if current prices are assigned a value of 240, this means that prices increased 140 percent over those of the base year, given that the base year bears a value of 100.

Money Supply and Its Velocity

The money supply is the total amount of a country's money that can be spent. This is comprised of currency and all types of bank deposits.

Prices will tend to rise when people are spending briskly and the money supply is constant. Conversely, prices will tend to fall when people are spending reluctantly and the money supply is constant. *Velocity* is the speed at which the money supply "turns over" or recirculates; the formula for velocity is

$$\text{Velocity} = \frac{\text{Gross national product}}{\text{Money supply}}$$

Business Cycles

In Ecclesiastes, it is said that there is "a time to laugh and a time to cry," "a time to reap and a time to sow." In economics, we observe that business activity often occurs in cycles over time, from "boom" to "bust" periods.

Inflation

Inflation is the state in which prices go up and buying power of currency goes down. (This doesn't mean that personal buying power goes down, because income may be rising faster than prices.) To (jokingly) quote Senator Alan Cranston, "Inflation is not all bad. After all, it has allowed every American to live in a more expensive neighborhood without moving." Inflation may be observed in any of three types:

- *Demand Pull*—happens with high levels of employment. When demand exceeds supply, prices go up: a "boom" period or, if you will, "good" inflation.

- *Change in Composition of Output*—happens when an economy shifts its emphasis to the creation and delivery of services rather than products. This is thought to be related to the notion that economies of scale for services are "exhausted" sooner than those for products (see the economies of scale discussion in Chapter 3).

- *Cost Push*—happens when supply diminishes relative to demand. This, in effect, increases demand and drives prices up. It is characterized by high unemployment and is especially dangerous when accompanied by "stagflation," increases in price in the absence of economic growth.

Recession

Recession is a major downturn in the economy, a "bust" period. Although criteria are subjective and vary considerably among economists, a commonly accepted criterion is two consecutive quarters with a decrease in growth (as measured in gross national product). A "domino effect" of sorts takes place when the downturn causes employers to cut costs, including those associated with labor. Such "downsizing," if anything, tends to fuel the recession further, in light of the understandable reluctance on the part of the unemployed to spend any more than is necessary.

Unfortunately, many businesses view economic downturns as periods in which they must cut costs and contract the range and magnitude of the activities in which they would normally be engaged. Actually, this perspective is shortsighted and usually not ultimately in the best interests of the organization. Recessions present a fine opportunity to address developmental areas, such as training. And although customers may be restrained relative to their normal buying behavior, marketers would be wise to "stay close" to the customer precisely at this critical point in time, for two important reasons. First, it may be possible to configure or reconfigure products and services to serve the particularly cost-conscious attitude of customers, such that business may be maintained to some degree or new market segments may emerge. Second (and figuratively speaking), the seeds that are planted today will produce fruit tomorrow. Of course, this is totally congruent with the orientation of customer focus, which should not cease simply because there is a hiatus or alteration in customer buying patterns.

In a similar vein, employers should be extremely reluctant to discharge skilled labor, even during economic downturns. It is often much harder to replace these individuals than is commonly anticipated.

Incidentally, observers seeking an indicator for the end of a downturn typically keep an eye on the corrugated box industry. When the shipping of boxes or cartons takes on a brisk pace, this suggests that recovery may be forthcoming.

Depression

A *depression* is a prolonged and extremely severe downturn in the economy. Usually precipitated by a stock market "crash," banks and other businesses fail. Production and investment are reduced to a very low level while unemployment soars.

Fiscal Policy Versus Monetary Policy

Economists differ among themselves as to the type of policy that should be implemented to spur economic growth. Advocates of fiscal policy believe that the government should rely heavily upon taxation as well as its spending. The latter commonly takes the form of transfer payments (for which no services or goods are actually given in return, such as unemployment benefits, Social Security, and Medicare/Medicaid coverage), infrastructure development projects (such as building of highways and hospitals), and investment in other programs.

In contrast, advocates of monetary policy believe that the government should affect desired change by means of altering the money supply and the interest rate. Yet these proponents find it disconcerting that they cannot forecast with any reliable degree of accuracy when actions taken by the Federal Reserve System will actually "kick in." So they would be content simply to have the Fed foster economic growth at a modest albeit roughly fixed rate.

The Federal Reserve System (specifically, the Federal Reserve Board) has as its objective the nation's economic well-being and tries to accomplish this on three fronts. It is actually a rather complicated system. The Federal Reserve Board (the "Fed"), a group of individuals who serve as the governing body of the Federal Reserve System performs the following functions:

1. Purchases Treasury bills if it wishes to stimulate the economy and sells them if it wishes to slow down economic growth that is either too extreme or that is accompanied by an unacceptably high rate of inflation.

2. Requires that banks maintain reserves against the loans they grant. The smaller the reserve requirement, the more money banks

are able to lend, and the greater the reserve requirement, the less money the banks are able to lend. The more money banks are able to lend, the greater the likelihood of economic growth. (The irony here is that many banks now have substantial reserves, but are reluctant to lend to any borrowers except the best credit risks. This helps to explain why recovery may be slow and incomplete.)

3. Acts as a bank to other banks, lending money to these entities at a preferred rate of interest, known as the discount rate. The lower the discount rate, the more money the banks are likely to borrow, and the more they borrow, the greater the likelihood of economic growth. When the discount rate is higher, banks tend to borrow less money, and there is less likelihood of economic growth.

The influence of the monetarists has been most strongly and most recently felt during the Reagan administration. Nobel laureate, Milton Friedman, essentially defined the movement in his pleas for a free market economy (i.e., laissez-faire or minimal government intervention). In some important respects, he walks in the footsteps of Adam Smith who, about two centuries earlier in his book, *The Wealth of Nations* (1776), espoused the notion of the "invisible hand," wherein Smith took the position that a business enterprise pursuing its own self-interest nonetheless serves the interests of society as well. So government should not interfere. Of course, both Smith and Friedman assume(d) that free competition always exists. (Obviously, neither could easily justify this stance in view of the reign of the "robber baron" monopolists at the turn of the twentieth century.) Both would also seem to favor what may be regarded as supply-side economics. This policy is skewed toward stimulation of production (i.e., supply) by means of tax incentives.

In contrast, the influence of those who favor fiscal policy was most evident during the two decades immediately preceding the Reagan presidency. The preeminent proponent of fiscal policy was John Maynard Keynes. His influence was so great that those who advocate fiscal policy are commonly referred to as Keynesians. Keynes, in his book, *General Theory of Employment, Interest and Money* (1936), contended that economic downturns could be prolonged and extended. Therefore, government should intervene by "fine-tuning," stimulating economic growth via spending and reducing taxes.[1]

Deficit in the National Budget

Simply put, the government spends more than it receives. As a result, future generations will have to bear the tax burden. In the United States, the vast majority of political responses call for an austerity program of some kind as a solution to the problem.

Foreign Trade

BALANCE OF PAYMENTS   The budget deficit is closely linked to the negative balance of payments in the United States. In other words, Americans buy more from foreign nations in the aggregate than foreign nations buy from the United States. Since deficits lead to devaluation of the dollar and lower currency exchange rates, the products that American firms export become less expensive abroad and the products that are imported to the United States become more expensive.

What causes a negative balance of payments? One explanation relates to the perception of the generally inferior quality of a nation's products within a certain product class or groups of product classes. For example, American quality in the manufacture of automobiles is widely regarded as poor by Japanese standards (see TQM in Chapter 3 on management) and Japanese demand for American cars is low. Others counter that the Japanese aren't buying American vehicles, not because of poor quality (as such), but because Japanese trade barriers close markets to foreign companies. Yet even those who might agree with this contention would have to admit that American marketers have often been grossly insensitive to differences in cultural preferences. For example, the American Motors Jeep is the first American-made car with a steering wheel on the right side to be sold in Japan. Why did American manufacturers persist (until 1993!) in making cars with steering wheels on the left side for the Japanese market which clearly preferred steering wheels on the right side?

THE INTERNATIONAL MONETARY SYSTEM   In 1941, the world's major economic players came together to foster international trade. Several years later, these nations established the World Bank and the International Monetary Fund (IMF), entities that grant credit to member countries and Third World nations for relatively high-risk undertakings and to other nations suffering unfavorable balance of payments (i.e., more funds leaving/spent by a nation than come into it/received by it).

MICROECONOMICS

Primary microeconomic concerns include analysis of

> Supply and demand
> Utility
> Productivity
> Nature of competition

Supply and Demand (Laws of)

The Supply Curve

The higher the price of a product or service, the greater the quantity of the item that producers will be willing to make available (i.e., supply), and conversely, the lower the price of a product or service, the smaller the quantity producers will be willing to make available (see Figure 5.1).

FIGURE 5.1   SUPPLY CURVE

The Demand Curve

The lower the price of a product or service, the greater the quantity of the item that consumers will be willing to buy (i.e., demand), and conversely, the higher the price of a product or service, the smaller the quantity consumers will be willing to buy (see Figure 5.2).

Equilibrium

Equilibrium is the point at which supply meets demand. More often than not, it represents an ideal rather than a truly attainable goal (see Figure 5.3).

Ceilings and Floors

Economic markets may be characterized by artificially imposed maximum (i.e., ceiling) and/or minimum (i.e., floor) supply and/or demand levels that interfere with the free market. For example, certain municipalities have enacted rent control laws (i.e., price ceilings), wherein landlords are required to keep residential rental levels below what, in effect, would be the "fair" market rate (i.e., equilibrium). As a result, many

FIGURE 5.2   DEMAND CURVE

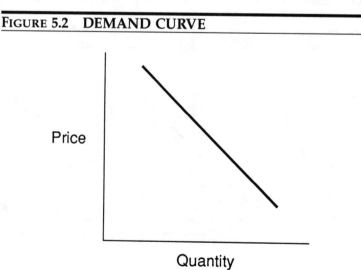

Price

Quantity

FIGURE 5.3   EQUILIBRIUM

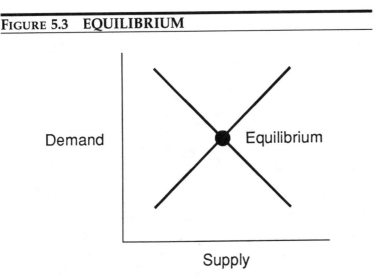

Demand   Equilibrium

Supply

of those dwelling units covered by rent control tend to be inhabited by individuals or families who would be forced to live elsewhere if they were required to pay the true market rate. Moreover, by taking rent-controlled units off the "regular" market (i.e., diminishing the supply of nonprotected housing), the demand for nonprotected housing is increased, and prices would reflect this.

Conversely, the federal government has enacted minimum wage laws (i.e., price floors), in which employers are required to compensate their workers at a certain minimum scale or at a higher level. By increasing the price of labor, demand for it diminishes and unemployment increases. Interestingly, during the first term of his presidency, Ronald Reagan proposed the creation of an "additional" and lower minimum wage level, to coexist with the incumbent minimum wage level. Reagan contended that application of this additional floor would be limited only to the "hard-core" unemployed, those who would not otherwise be able to find work. Employers, he reasoned, would have an incentive to hire these individuals, since the price of labor would be perceived as "artificially" low. Moreover, benefits in the form of new skills, along with a work ethic and a salary, would ensure to those hired, as well. And, of course, unemployment would drop. (The plan was not adopted.)

Elasticity of Demand

The degree to which demand for a product or service can be altered by a change in price indicates the extent of the elasticity of such demand. For example, a person who seeks to purchase a particular brand and model of automobile may decide to shop competitively from dealer to dealer for the lowest price. This would characterize demand that is elastic. However, there are circumstances where the level of demand is not altered by a change in price. For example, a person who is diabetic will probably be willing to pay as much money as he or she has to buy insulin, the medication that would sustain that individual's life. In this case, the demand is inelastic.

By the way, this latter example has ominous implications as it pertains, for example, to the tobacco industry. The price of cigarettes has increased by about 5 percent every six months over the last few years. As long as the tobacco industry can get away with this while at the same time enhancing production efficiencies (and it does), it will be able continually to reap huge profits, even in the face of diminishing sales levels.

Cross-elasticity of Demand

Cross-elasticity describes the effect that an alteration in the price of one item will have on the demand for another item. If the items are complements (such as peanut butter and jelly), a dramatic increase in the price of one item will be followed by a diminution in the price of the other. If, however, the items are substitutes (such as tea and coffee) and the price of one item goes up dramatically, consumers may switch to the lower-priced item.

Diminishing Marginal Utility (Law of)

This concept or economic "law" posits that the level of demand or "satisfaction" derived from a product or service diminishes with each additional unit consumed until no further benefit is perceived, within a given time frame. This would help to explain the underlying marketing strategy of Schaeffer beer, whose slogan, "Schaeffer is the one beer to have when you're having more than one," implied that the rate at which marginal utility of this brand declines is slower than it would be with competing brands and this might be an ample selling point for heavy users. Therefore, marketers would be wise to conduct research to ascertain the quantity of a product that the consumer is likely to "be satisfied with" and buy within a given time frame. Having done so, the product can be packaged in a quantity or configuration designed to maximize the consumer's sense of utility.

Diminishing Returns (Law of)

This concept suggests that although additional units of labor may contribute to increased productivity in absolute numbers, each such additional unit contributes relatively less than the preceding unit to this productivity. Why? Because there are fewer machines, tools, or other inputs per worker.[2] (As you might imagine, this is a countervailing factor to economies of scale.)

Comparative Advantage (Paradox of)

It is in the interest of a nation to import an item from another nation when it cannot produce the item as inexpensively. The concept of comparative advantage goes a step farther, contending that it may be to a country's advantage to import goods from other nations even though they may be able to produce the goods less expensively at home. This is based upon the premise that not producing the item in favor of producing another item which offers better production efficiencies will ultimately benefit both countries (see the economies of scale discussion in Chapter 3).[3]

Zero Sum Game

This concept was originally introduced by noted mathematician John von Neumann and more recently popularized by economist Lester Thurow of M.I.T. Simply put, ZSG implies that for each economic "player" who gains a certain sum, another player must lose an equal sum (see the game theory discussion in Chapter 8). Enlightened managers may try to avoid zero-sum games, preferring instead the notion of "win-win" situations, in which one party need not lose for the other to gain. However, in a world where economic players vie for their slices of a finite pie, ZSG characterizes redistribution of income via taxation as well as that of employee compensation.

Satisficing

Herbert Simon, the Nobel laureate, is most closely associated with this term. Essentially, Simon's contribution may be abstracted to suggest that the maximum or "the most" is not necessarily as good as the optimum or "the best."[4] For example, an organization that wins so much market share that it faces antitrust action and ultimately dissolution is clearly not as well off as another organization that claims a lesser market share but focuses more so on profitability. In this light, we might opt to "satisfice" or optimize rather than maximize.

THE ECONOMICS CHECKLIST

1. Can I be more proactive in anticipating changes in business cycles?

2. Does pricing of my products adequately address supply and demand concerns, such as elasticity?

3. Does the configuration or packaging of my products maximize utility for my customers?

4. Which of my business activities are zero sum game in nature and which are not? Can I change this? Do I want to? Is it in my interest to do so?

5. How do economic factors reframe the way I view competition?

RECOMMENDED READING

Bach, George L., *Economics* (Englewood Cliffs, NJ: Prentice Hall, 1987).

Baumol, William J., and Alan S. Blinder, *Economics: Principles and Policy* (New York: Harcourt Brace Jovanovich, 1991).

Casler, Stephen D., *Introduction to Economics* (New York: Harper-Collins, 1992).

Silk, Leonard, *Economics in Plain English* (New York: Simon & Schuster, 1978).

ORGANIZATIONS AND RESOURCES

American Economic Association
1313 21st Avenue S
Nashville, TN 37212
(615) 322-2595

National Association of Business Economists
28790 Chagrin Boulevard, Suite 300
Cleveland, OH 44122
(216) 464-7986

ENDNOTES

1. Susan Lee, *Susan Lee's ABZs of Economics* (New York: Pocket Books, 1987).
2. Stephen D. Casler, *Introduction to Economics* (New York: HarperCollins, 1992).
3. William J. Baumol and Alan S. Blinder, *Economics: Principles and Policy* (New York: Harcourt Brace Jovanovich, 1991).
4. Susan Lee, *Susan Lee's ABZs of Economics*.

CHAPTER 6

TECHNOLOGY
MANAGEMENT

The computer has revolutionized our culture and the way we do business. It has been posited that, if the aircraft industry had grown as rapidly as the computer industry has in the recent past, the Concorde would now carry as many as 10,000 passengers at more than 60 times the speed of sound and the fare would cost far less than $1.00 per passenger.

Although computer technology has certainly proven to be extremely valuable and powerful in its own right, melding the computer with other technologies facilitates even more impressive synergies and exponential growth opportunities (see Figure 6.1). The following represents applications that are, for the most part, widely employed. Asterisks (*) denote applications that might more aptly appear under the heading "The Shape of Things to Come." This latter category speaks to the future. However, the pace of change is so rapid that technological advances come, and in some cases, will have gone sooner than we expected.

FIGURE 6.1   COMBINATION OF TECHNOLOGIES TO DRAW UPON SYNERGIES

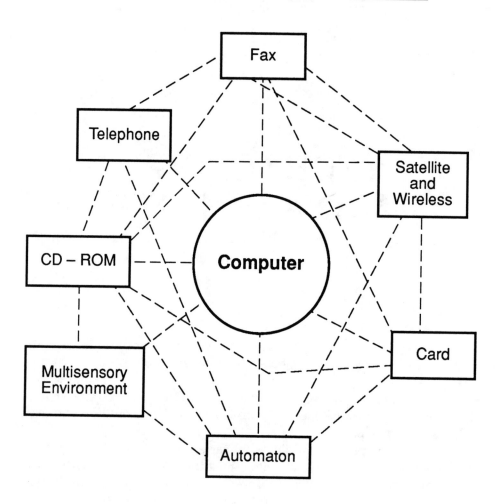

COMPUTER (STAND ALONE)

Artificial Intelligence (AI) facilitates the analysis of problems and identification of their solutions. *Knowledge-based systems (KBS)* do so by searching for a historical match (i.e., a previous instance or case) and employing *case-based reasoning (CBR)*. *Expert systems (ES)* equal or exceed human intelligence. Artificial intelligence allows the computer to serve as an "advisor" of sorts to the user. It is this "human" characteristic of AI that is so appealing and holds such great promise.

AI can be used in the formulation of business strategies. It can, for example, evaluate macroenvironmental factors or market conditions as well as internal strengths and weaknesses, identify core problems, and suggest the appropriate remedies and plans of action. Some of the bigger securities firms use AI to forecast market patterns and the performance of stocks and bonds.

The medical field was among the first to use successfully a version of AI (more specifically, ES). The physician is able to share the patient's family history and self-reported and empirically observed symptoms with the computer, which, in turn, identifies a probable diagnosis, a probable prognosis, and a suggested course of action (or choice of options) to treat the individual. An important human resources implication of ES is that less skilled personnel can be used to perform what would otherwise be regarded as more advanced and difficult tasks. For example, a nurse might be capable of performing the preliminary diagnosis and prognosis, freeing the physician to perform emergency surgery.

Computer-assisted design (CAD) allows architects and designers to automate much of the creative process. At the press of a button, the professional is able to alter dimensions/aspect ratios, shapes, colors, and other variables of a design and generate an almost instantaneous hard copy of the work into a blueprint or similar tangible form.

Computer-based training (CBT) allows the individual to learn at his or her own particular pace, using interactive processes.

Computer-assisted software engineering (CASE) allows the computer-literate professional to work in tandem with the content expert to create software programs relating to the latter's field of expertise.

Word processing (WP) allows the user to employ the computer to create text, as one would do with a typewriter. In fact, many word processing programs are also capable of producing a wide variety of typefaces and graphics (i.e., icons, borders, special characters). Textual and stylistic changes can be made quickly and easily.

Desktop publishing (DTP) allows the individual to create printed materials of high technical quality, eliminating the need to send the work out to graphic designers, typesetters, and related professionals. In fact, graphic designers themselves along with their related professionals now employ this technology as the industry standard. Many typesetters (i.e., those who lay "cold" type) have adopted the technology or have been forced out of business due to obsolescence. Practical applications of DTP include the design of magazines, newsletters, reports, and many types of presentations.

Spreadsheets allow management decision makers to evaluate and/or calculate possible outcomes under a multitude of scenarios by automated representation of matrixed rows and columns. Each "cell" (i.e., point where a row meets a column) provides data. In fact, one can (at the press of a key) instantly "create" a new or hypothetical scenario (i.e., "what if . . .") at will.

Data base management (DBM) allows the business enterprise to optimally organize and compile information for its operational and strategic purposes. DBM is the structured collection of information. It automatically maintains defined data relationships. "Infopreneurship," or the selling of specialized and proprietary information, is a particularly interesting and appealing phenomenon, since it is marked by rapid growth and market entry is relatively easy.

COMPUTER COMBINED WITH TELEPHONE

Electronic mail (E-mail) allows the user to send (and receive) written communications to other individuals with computers who are linked via telephone lines to the same E-mail system. This allows individuals to send or receive instantaneously a "broadcast letter," one that is capable of reaching many people.

Electronic data interchange (EDI) enables disintermediation, which obsoletes third parties or intermediaries traditionally required for facilitation of transactions. EDI portends serious consequences for the banking industry as we know it, since financial institutions would no longer be necessary for check clearance. Moreover, transactions can be effected instantaneously. Proctor & Gamble has an EDI system in place with the Wal-Mart retail chain, allowing P&G to know when inventory levels of the products it supplies to Wal-Mart stores are running low. Once this mechanism is "triggered," it then automatically reorders and simultaneously sets in motion the shipping and invoicing processes.

Automated voice response (AVR) allows for automated and interactive communication (e.g., "press 1 for . . . , press 2 for . . ."). This can facilitate important tasks, including automated payroll processing and order taking. Voice mail systems have become even more popular. However, a widespread criticism relates to customers calling an organization and often getting trapped in "voice jail" or a looped system that leads back to where the individual started or to a dead end wherein none of the options offered to the caller is applicable or desirable. Aside from taking greater care in the design of systems, the organization can minimize this problem simply by making a live, human voice available if the caller so desires (e.g., "press 0 for Operator").

"700" prefix telephone numbers will allow people to avoid playing "telephone tag" and missing each other's calls by acquiring a permanent, lifetime long-distance telephone number that begins with the area code "700" and can be accessed anywhere the individual travels. (*)

"800" prefix telephone numbers allow people to call toll-free or at no charge, dialing a telephone number that begins with the area code "800." The perceived value of toll-free calling to both the consumer as well as marketer can be substantial, since it is congruent with a customer focus orientation. Moreover, it is far less expensive for the marketer than is commonly realized, and research indicates that listing of a toll-free number tends to enhance an organization's perceived reliability and credibility in the minds of consumers.

"900" prefix telephone numbers allow marketers to use a telephone line to generate revenues in return for providing information or entertainment services, such as stock market quotations/news, sports updates, horoscopes, and personal/psychological advice. Callers are usually charged per minute on line and may incur minimum charges.

The primary advantages of "900" for the entrepreneur or corporation include ease of collection (charges appear on customers' telephone bills) and instantaneous market research (effectiveness of advertising can be gauged and media tactics can be adjusted quickly).

"1000" prefix telephone numbers, a vision of futurist Faith Popcorn, will allow callers to receive a customized version of "900" service. For example, an experienced plumber could be available to "talk you through" repair of your kitchen faucet. (*)[1]

Videoconferencing links people via television screens from two or more remote locations. This technology can turn a meeting into an event, and is probably the next best thing to being there in person. It is widely regarded as somewhat expensive. It is, nonetheless, associated with cost reduction, since people can be brought together to "meet" without actually having to travel to a remote location. Travel and lodging expenses are, therefore, kept to a minimum or completely avoided. And, of course, executive time (keeping in mind that "time is money") is not wasted traveling, as well. Intel, a progressive and impressive "cutting-edge" user of technology, is now employing *desktop videoconferencing,* using PCs to send and receive audio/video signals to interconnect employees and others at their workstations. In a similar vein, Intel and others link groups of employees (often field sales personnel) from pay telephones! Hence, the term "quick (tele)conferencing."

COMPUTER COMBINED WITH FACSIMILE

Multiple transmission transforms fax into a mass medium, much as E-mail can "broadcast" text. Given the ever-improving quality of fax (including regular rather than thermal paper as well as color capability), facsimiles may come and be used and viewed as newsletters or even newspapers. This raises the issue of unsolicited fax or "junk fax," in the same vein as "junk mail" has posed a problem. Many organizations are inundated with unsolicited and unwanted facsimile communications (typically transmitted overnight, when telephone rates go down). So they have responded by shutting off their machines after hours or by providing access codes only to those parties from whom they wish to receive fax communications (*selective reception*).

COMPUTER COMBINED WITH SATELLITE/WIRELESS

Over-the-air distribution allows us to receive services such as "canned" music (e.g., Muzak). The transition from cassette delivery to over-the-air delivery greatly reduces or eliminates costs (i.e., cassette duplication, shipping). The technology also exists to transmit feature motion pictures in this manner. (*)

The Taco Bell fast-food chain employs wireless technology to speed up the taking and processing of orders when many people or cars are queued up and waiting to be served. An employee will fan out to the line, entering orders into a hand-held device that transmits them over the air to a screen above the food preparation area in the kitchen.

Wireless data communication will allow you to sit under a tree, create a document on your laptop computer, and send it via radio signal to a remote location. There, it can be printed in desktop quality and transmitted as a facsimile (if you wish) to other users and destinations.[2]

COMPUTER WITH INTERNET

Originally developed to minimize any disruption in communication in the event of nuclear war, the Internet has come to play an important role in many socio-cultural areas, including education and entertainment, and, of course, in commerce, as well. Those who "surf the 'net" can "visit a Web site," allowing them to learn about a company's products and services and actually even place an order over the 'net via credit card. (Security problems regarding credit card fraud have been greatly reduced and will be even less of an issue in the future).

COMPUTER COMBINED WITH AUTOMATON

Computer-assisted manufacturing (CAM) allows manufacturers to avoid placing human lives in jeopardy, as with nuclear and other hazardous materials. Proponents of robotics would also be quick to tell you that robots do not make nearly as many errors as human beings, are capable of performing surprisingly delicate tasks, can work virtually 24 hours a day (minus maintenance time), and never complain.

COMPUTER COMBINED WITH CARD

The *smart card* allows organizations to use credit card technology (i.e., card incorporating microchip technology) to automate transactions and record keeping.

While on a recent business trip to Dallas, a friend drove me to a meeting. As we approached a booth to pay the highway toll, I expected that she would gradually slow down to pay the attendant. Instead, she shot through the toll booth at about 50 miles per hour. I was shocked by the notion that she had "run" a toll and fully expected police cars with sirens blaring to follow in hot pursuit. My fears were calmed when my friend explained that she had a "toll tag" (i.e., smart card) on her windshield, which registered automatically each time she passed a toll checkpoint and that she received a monthly statement for all such toll charges.

Cards with internal memory would also enable physicians, for example, by processing a patient's card, to receive a detailed family history as well as a personal history of conditions, medications taken, and more.

COMPUTER COMBINED WITH SENSORY OR MULTISENSORY ENVIRONMENT

Virtual reality (VR) allows the individual to don a special apparatus which introduces him to enter a "make-believe" multisensory environment. Can you imagine being "inside" or part of a video game in addition to just being a player at the controls? or going on a scenic tour of Europe without leaving your hometown? or displaying and demonstrating your entire product line for customers in a showroom that doesn't actually exist? Early inroads into VR were made by NASA in the form of simulations or "games" to train pilots.[4] The medical profession also pioneered use of the technology to simulate a wide variety of surgical situations. This would enable the med student to make an "incision" into the semblance of a human body and, if the "scalpel" motion were incorrect and nicked a "blood vessel," "blood" would actually spurt, a very realistic training method. (*)

Ubiquitous computing (UC) will allow individuals to utilize and interface seemingly low-tech office tools such as notepads and blackboards which have computer intelligence built into them and are able to generate and send information. (*)

This is congruent with the vision of the "paperless office," wherein physical storage space of information is kept to a minimum and access to this information is quick.

As you can see, the possibilities are almost endless. For example, a wireless computer (utilizing cellular technology) that also functions as a remote fax machine and remote telephone is soon to be widely available. How about the melding of artificial intelligence with virtual reality? Buck Rogers, move over!

MANAGEMENT INFORMATION SYSTEMS

Management information systems (MISs) are designed to provide management with information for optimal decision making. This suggests the creation and maintenance of a wide variety of data bases or bodies of information in such virtually all functional categories, including but certainly not limited to marketing, finance, human resources, research and development, and strategic planning. And to the extent that "knowledge is power," MIS can be a powerful asset. Therefore, many organizations that make a serious commitment to the MIS function actually appoint a chief information officer (or CIO) to oversee its operation, just as a chief executive officer (or CEO) is ultimately responsible for the entire organization.

At its inception, MIS was mainframe based and, therefore, largely centralized. While its potential is great, the opportunity for inefficiency—or worse—tends to arise when the information technology specialists ("techies") who operate the system fail to provide management ("users") with information that is relevant and timely and is conveyed in a manner or format that is easily understood and usable. For this reason, the linkage of personal computers (PC) by local area networks (LAN) has become very popular. This allows managers to pull information from the mainframe in a more "user-friendly" manner and to share information more easily among each other. Note: Technology managers are still necessary to design the infrastructure for MIS. A key function of these professionals is to prevent uploading data from PC to mainframe without proper controls. Otherwise, the integrity of the "books" can be jeopardized or "corrupted."

THE HIGH-TECH CHALLENGE TO MANAGEMENT

In light of the rapid change that characterizes high technology, there are numerous issues, opportunities, and obstacles that decision makers have been forced to address. These include the following:

Finance

Often, the pace of technological breakthroughs outstrips the schedule for recoupment of investments in a given technology (see depreciation, ROI, NPV, IRR and payback in Chapter 2 on accounting and finance). So the organization must decide whether to upgrade to state of the art even though the cost of the incumbent technology would not yet have been fully justified or to "stay the course" with the intention of meeting its original financial plans, although delay in embracing a new generation may render the company less competitive or otherwise cause it to forgo opportunities for substantial cost reduction or revenue generation that would more than offset the cost of upgrading.

Marketing

We must weigh the trade-off of automation against personalization and the human touch (high tech versus high touch). Ultimately, customer focus is often the deciding factor.

Early research indicated that approximately 33 percent of the entire universe of financial services customers resisted using *automated teller machines (ATM)* and presumably other high-tech equipment.[5] (Current anecdotal reports suggest that we adjust this figure to 20 percent.) These people fear or are simply uncomfortable with technology. They demand or require a "high-touch" or human approach. Service providers would prefer that customers use the ATMs rather than human tellers, since automated processing of transactions is less expensive. So, in the interest of satisfying these technophobic customers while trying to get them to accept and use ATM machines, some imaginative service providers have equipped their ATMs with audio-video terminals that link the user to a specially trained human teller who can walk them through the procedure. This enables the hesitant user to "give it a try" and, once comfortable with the technology, continue using the machines without assistance.

Human Resources

Just as financial plans must be reappraised, the deployment of human capital must be adequate to introduce, operate, and maintain high-tech systems. Unfortunately, management and employees don't always understand how to use equipment efficiently. This may be attributed, to a large extent, to the lack of proper training. In addition, "techies" have long been criticized for failing to understand the user's actual needs and preferences; they simply "don't know the business." They must see the business through the eyes of their internal client or user, anticipate questions or concerns reflecting the user's particular orientation, and provide information before it is actually requested. In fact, they might even offer suggestions regarding ways that information can best be used. For example, a technology manager serving an internal client or user in the marketing department might anticipate his client's focus on segmentation and take the liberty of organizing databases toward that end. He might even include comments or recommendations as to which market segments are likely to be worth targeting. Serving a user in the finance department would, of course, shift the focus. In anticipation of investment analysis concerns, the technology manager might, for example, offer to provide information couched in terms of NPV, IRR, and payback— before it is specifically requested.

Another important human resources issue involves the contention that heavy utilization of technology may actually be explained as undue dependence on it. The late Calvin Pava, foremost expert on office design, warned against such overdependence. He stated that the effect of technology on human behavior can be to "engender passivity" and to stunt human potential.[6] If his theory is correct, the dilemma arises as to where exactly to draw the line between proper use and abuse.

Engineering/Security

The deployment of backup systems to avoid loss in the face of catastrophes is absolutely essential. Consider, if you will, the tremendous damage done in September 1991 when AT&T's long distance telephone system "went down" due to equipment failure. In a similar vein, unauthorized access to computer systems by "hackers" and the introduction of "viruses," which destroy or distort information, underscore the need for sophisticated security measures.

Ethics and the Law

(See the section in Chapter 7 dealing with privacy and informed consent.)

Strategic Planning

Due to the large capital outlays that may be necessary for high-technology research and development (as well as marketing), strategic partnerships or co-ventures with other organizations, perhaps even with those traditionally viewed as competitors, may make sense. For example, Apple Computer's strategic alliance with Sony is responsible for the great success of Apple's Powerbook computers. The two organizations enjoy a powerful synergy, in that Apple is recognized for its strength in developing user-friendly or easy-to-understand computers, while Sony is acknowledged for its prowess at manufacturing miniaturized electronic products. Both entities operate globally.

PROGRESS THROUGH TECHNOLOGY?

Well, not necessarily. In fact, productivity may actually decline due to the following:

Poor Training

Users don't understand how to employ equipment efficiently.

Poor Procedures and Systems

"Techies" don't design systems intelligently because "they don't know the business" (see the human resources discussion in "The High-Tech Challenge to Management" section earlier in this chapter).

Poor Equipment

Hardware or software is inherently flawed.

This clearly indicates that the acquisition and nominal operation of high-ticket and high-tech equipment is just the tip of the iceberg, insofar as the technology manager is concerned. Now, he or she must "manage" the technology as well as personnel. Responsibilities must include training, setting and maintaining procedural standards for operation, and assuring the integrity of the equipment itself.

TECHNOLOGY MANAGEMENT CHECKLIST

1. What constitutes "state of the art" in my field?

2. Am I making use of these technologies?

3. Can I combine technologies to enjoy synergies?

4. How can I minimize the potential pitfalls associated with the introduction or upgrading of technology?

5. How does technology influence the way I manage people?

6. Can I better balance "high-tech" and "high-touch" considerations?

RECOMMENDED READING

Edosomwan, Johnson A., *Integrating Innovation and Technology Management* (New York: John Wiley and Sons, 1989).

Monger, Rod F., *Mastering Technology* (New York: The Free Press, 1988).

ORGANIZATIONS AND RESOURCES

Association of Computer Users
P.O. Box 2189
Berkeley, CA 94702
(415) 549-4336

Association of Electronic Cottagers
P.O. Box 1738
Davis, CA 95617
(No telephone number available)

International Interactive Communications Society
2298 Valerie Court
Campbell, CA 95008
(408) 866-7941

ENDNOTES

1. Faith Popcorn, *The Popcorn Report* (New York: Doubleday, 1991).
2. Robert E. Calem, "Look, No Wires! But the Pages Fly!" *The New York Times*, November 8, 1992.
3. Cathy Hilborn, "Brave New Disks," *Financial Times of Canada*, November 28, 1992.
4. Steve Ditlea, "Virtual Reality Virtually Here," *Hemispheres*, October 1992.
5. Rod F. Monger, *Mastering Technology* (New York: The Free Press, 1988).
6. Calvin Pava, *Managing New Office Technology: An Organizational Strategy* (New York: The Free Press, 1983).

CHAPTER 7

BUSINESS POLICY
AND ETHICS

Ethics is the code of conduct or system of moral principles by which we lead our lives and carry out our business. In light of a proliferation of well-publicized, unethical behavior in the workplace and in the marketplace as well, business schools have slowly responded to the need to provide ethical guidance and education for students and executives. It is ironic and tragic that those who need to be educated in ethics the most are typically those who would claim that they don't need it at all, while those who actively seek guidance in this area are typically those who actually need it the least. For this reason, business schools are wise to offer ethics courses as mandatory core offerings rather than electives.

Although some take the position that the teaching of ethics should be conducted in Sunday School rather than the executive suite, they might do well to ponder that ethical business behavior is ultimately cost effective.[1] Consider, if you will, the legal expenses and monetary damages that can arise from unethical behavior, not to mention lowered employee morale and, ultimately, the loss of customers.

FORMULATION OF ETHICAL STANDARDS

The formulation of ethical standards can be difficult. After all, ethics deals in terms of rights and obligations, and the perception of these is both subjective and qualitative. In contrast, analysis of investments in terms of their potential risks and rewards can be viewed rather more objectively and quantitatively.

And to whom is the ethical business manager responsible? Truly, the manager must serve numerous stakeholders (see Figure 7.1). These groups include employees (individually and collectively in the form of unions), customers, suppliers, competitors, stockholders, and various governmental and communal entities (local, national, and global). So what does the manager do when the interests of these stakeholders are at variance with one another (as is often the case)? For example, closing a marginally profitable manufacturing plant in a community that is heavily dependent upon the company for its employment must be weighed against the ability to cut costs to maximize returns for stockholders.

General Guidelines

There is no single correct or "cookie-cutter" solution. However, the decision maker has to weigh the five points listed here,[2] keeping in mind the trade-off of costs and benefits:

1. The nature of "good" or "bad" that is in question

2. The urgency of the circumstances

3. The certainty of a particular outcome

4. The intensity of one's influence on the outcome

5. The availability of alternative means

When in doubt, trade and professional associations can be valuable resources in the formulation of ethical business codes. On a personal note and "off the record," I would like to suggest an unscientific method for helping to make difficult ethical decisions, which, I believe, can be valuable to all but those with sociopathic tendencies.

FIGURE 7.1 STAKEHOLDER INTERESTS FACING THE MANAGER

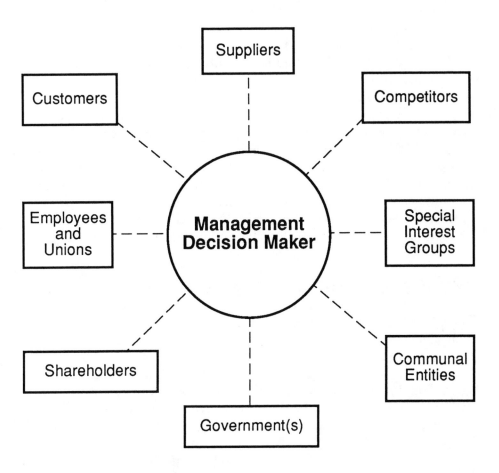

After weighing decision options, the individual should ask himself or herself the following "litmus test" question: "Would I be ashamed (not just embarrassed) to read the news of my decision on the front page of my hometown newspaper, where all my family, friends, neighbors, and business associates will know about it?"

If the answer is "no," the decision is probably okay. The value of this exercise points to the need for executives to keep in touch with their true selves, to trust their visceral responses and further develop their intuition.

How does law relate to ethics? In principle, the laws of a society reflect its ethical standards. In practice, however, ethical standards often supersede legal standards. For example, it is not against the law in many jurisdictions to terminate an employee "at will." In other words, an employer may do so "without cause" or, if you will, just because he or she feels like it. Ethical standards suggest that an employee may be terminated only for "just cause" (i.e., a good reason, such as stealing or substance abuse on the job or if survival of the business enterprise is endangered).

APPLICATION TO SPECIFIC BUSINESS ISSUES

The following business "issues" are among the most important and commonly encountered, but by no means represent a complete set of legal and ethical guidelines for management decision making and behavior.

I suggest that for definitive and authoritative legal guidelines, managers would be well advised to refer to their employer's "Officer's Manual" (i.e., formalized code of behavior) or consult with the organization's staff attorneys or legal counsel. (Legal obligations may differ by jurisdiction and may change as a result of challenges in the courts. They should be viewed as "generalizations" and will be considered from comparative legal and ethical perspectives (in alphabetical order):

Advertising, Truth in

If an advertisement has the effect of being deceptive, it is unethical, regardless of its intent. Law supports this position, but enforcement may be lacking in stringency.

Bribery

Bribery is action on the part of an employee to permit a third party to gain unfair advantage in dealings with his firm in return for being enriched in some way (e.g., kickbacks). This is both unethical and illegal.

Confidentiality

It is unethical for organizations to release confidential information about their employees or customers to third parties without express permission. If such information was originally obtained by the firm with the understanding that it would be kept confidential, then disclosure to third parties might constitute breach of an implied contract and subject the company to payment of damages under civil law. Failure by professionals (e.g., lawyers, physicians, psychologists) to honor confidentiality is not only unethical and illegal (under civil law), but may also subject them to revocation of licensure or other sanctions.

Conflict of Interest

In this condition, an individual may enrich himself or herself at the expense of his or her employer or client. For example, the manager who hires her husband's catering firm to handle her employer's Christmas party may be creating a conflict of interests. The rule of thumb in these matters involves the element of concealment. Legally, conflict of interest does not exist if the party makes full disclosure regarding the potential for conflicts. If, for example, the manager revealed in advance to her boss that the catering firm she planned to hire was owned by her husband, that would not constitute a conflict. It might, however, be regarded as poor judgment.

Denigration

To spread false and damaging information about a competitor is both unethical and illegal, subjecting the offender to damages under civil law. If the claims are true, however, such action would remain within the bounds of legal behavior while ethical status would be problematic. The consideration here hinges upon the contention that infliction of harm upon a competitor may harm the entire industry.[3]

Discrimination

Bias against individuals on the basis of race, ethnicity, creed, age, gender, or sexual orientation is unethical and illegal. Aside from being morally reprehensible, it is also irrational. For example, the manager who fails to promote an individual on the basis of prejudice is underdeploying the firm's human capital.

Firing Employees

From a legal standpoint, whether a termination is rightful may depend upon whether it is based upon "at will" (i.e., employer's discretion or whim) or "just cause" (i.e., employer's justification) considerations. Generally, discrimination cannot justify termination. From an ethical standpoint, however, employers may not fire "at will," and employees are entitled to due process, the opportunity to state their case and be judged fairly (i.e., overruling a biased or unfair immediate boss). If they are terminated, it is the employer's ethical if not legal obligation to obviate the damage inflicted (e.g., via severance, outplacement services).

Gifts

Since gifts are things of value, they can be used to obtain unfair advantage (see "Bribery"). However, the normative standards for "stepping over the line" can vary dramatically. For example, many government agencies, as a matter of formal policy, do not even permit their employees to accept a cup of coffee free of charge from potential vendors, whereas executives in the entertainment industry are often wined and dined in fine restaurants at vendor expense. As a rule of thumb, many organizations have established the policy that allows managers to accept gifts of "nominal value" (widely regarded as under $25 in value) and requires them to return items of greater value tactfully or obtain permission to accept these from superiors or "integrity officers."

Ignorance of the Law

Simply put, it does not constitute a justification or defense from a legal or ethical standpoint.

Informed Consent

If a party to a business relationship is put at risk as a result of performance under the terms of this relationship, it can reasonably expect to be informed in advance of the risks thereto appertaining. For example, the buyer of a product is entitled to know the real or potential dangers involved in using that product (and these can be listed on the label and/or in an accompanying pamphlet). If the consumer then knowingly purchases the item, consent is implied. Failure to obtain informed consent is unethical and may subject the offender to damages under civil law.

Moonlighting

Generally, moonlighting (i.e., working at a part-time job, "on the side") is neither unethical nor illegal. It may become an issue where the employer specifically prohibits it and/or where the "other" job is with a competitor, supplier, or customer (in other words, where the potential for conflict of interest is real).

Price Cutting

The deciding factor is intent. Cutting price to dispose of inventory would not be unethical, whereas doing so to undercut the competition would be. Price cutting is not, in and of itself, illegal.

Price Fixing

Conspiracy by "competitors" to set prices is both unethical and illegal.[4]

Privacy

Privacy is a right, legally as well as ethically. If your actions will cause the violation of someone's privacy, you must inform the individual of your intent, explain the risks involved, and obtain the party's consent (see "Informed Consent").

Report, Obligation to

Employees who have *suspicion* of an unethical activity are not ethically obligated to report it. If there is *knowledge* of such an activity, ethical obligation to report it would be discretionary and would depend upon the individual's cost-benefit analysis. While suspicion of a crime does not legally obligate an employee to report it, knowledge of a crime (before or after the fact) does call for the individual to come forward. Failure to do so may cause the individual to be regarded under the law as an accomplice or accessory to the crime.[5]

Sexual Harassment

Unequivocally, unwelcome sexual advances or coercion is unethical and illegal.

Whistle Blowing

(See Report, Obligation to.)

CONTRACTS

While ethical codes help us to establish standards governing the rights and obligations that exist in business relationships, these standards can be translated into agreements known as contracts. Parties to a contract exchange promises. These may be express (i.e., communicated explicitly and clearly, either in verbal or written form) or implied (i.e., deduced from actions or behavior). Proper contracts involve the following conditions:[6]

1. One party makes an offer which is accepted by the other party.

2. Each party must offer the other consideration (i.e., something of value) in return for what it is to receive from the other party.

3. Both parties must act of their own free will, free of duress and undue influence.

4. The agreement cannot include fraudulent claims or representations.

5. The agreement cannot be in violation of the law.

6. Certain types of contracts must be in written form (e.g., those involving real estate).

ALTERNATIVE DISPUTE RESOLUTION (ADR)

What happens when disputes arise from contracts? Litigation (i.e., fighting it out in court) can be extremely time consuming and expensive, often involving years of legal processes and millions of dollars spent and, arguably, wasted. The following alternative dispute resolution (ADR) methods are increasing in popularity, because they can be conducted in a matter of a few days and at a minute fraction of litigation cost:

Arbitration

The parties argue their case before impartial referees or judges (i.e., arbitrators) under the sponsorship of an organization such as the American Arbitration Association. They mutually agree to be bound by the decision of the arbitrators (i.e., binding arbitration). There is no right of appeal if things don't go your way.

Mediation

The parties argue their case before impartial referees or judges (i.e., mediators). However, they are not required to accept the decision.

Minitrial

The parties argue their case before a panel of "judges" gathered from both sides of the dispute (e.g., executives employed by each organization) and moderated by an impartial guide. These settlement proceedings are not formal and do not require adherence to rules of evidence. The judges typically arrive at a solution, with or without the participation of the impartial guide.[7]

Note: Strategically, litigation may be a preferred remedy when one litigant plans to win a legal "war of attrition." For example, a large corporation with vast financial and other resources might enjoy a decided advantage over a "little guy" who may not be able to afford a protracted court battle. On the other hand, a large but image-conscious corporation might prefer ADR, viewing it as a means of minimizing adverse publicity.

THE BUSINESS POLICY AND ETHICS CHECKLIST

1. Am I able to articulate, formulate, and feel comfortable with a set of ethical standards?

2. Do I have a better understanding of how to deal with particular business and workplace issues from an ethical standpoint?

3. How do I feel about ethics as it relates to law?

4. How does a contract address ethical as well as legal concerns?

5. What alternatives do I have to resolution of disputes through the court system?

RECOMMENDED READING

Beauchamp, Tom L., *Case Studies in Business, Society and Ethics* (Englewood Cliffs, NJ: Prentice Hall, 1983).

Bowie, Norman, *Business Ethics* (Englewood Cliffs, NJ: Prentice Hall, 1982).

Garrett, Thomas A., and Richard J. Klonoski, *Business Ethics* (Englewood Cliffs, NJ: Prentice Hall, 1986).

Rion, Michael, *The Responsible Manager* (New York: AMACON, 1986).

Solomon, Robert, and Kristine R. Hanson, *Above the Bottom Line: An Introduction to Business Ethics* (New York: Harcourt Brace Jovanovich, 1983).

ORGANIZATIONS AND RESOURCES

Academy of Ethical Studies
117 W. Harrison Building, 6th floor
Suite I-104
Chicago, IL 60605
(800) 423-3844

Ethics Resource Center
600 New Hampshire Ave., N.W.
Suite 400
Washington, D.C. 20037
(202) 333-3419

Society for Business Ethics
Loyola University of Chicago,
Dept. of Philosophy
6525 N. Sheridan Road
Chicago, IL 60626
(312) 508-2725

ENDNOTES

1. Robert C. Solomon and Kristine Hanson, *It's Good Business* (New York: Atheneum, 1985).
2. Thomas M. Garrett and Richard J. Klonoski, *Business Ethics* (Englewood Cliffs, NJ: Prentice Hall, 1986).

3. Ibid.

4. Ibid.

5. Ibid.

6. Donald A. Wiesner and Nicholas A. Glaskowsky, *Theory and Problems of Business Law* (New York: McGraw-Hill, 1985).

7. Tamar Lewin, "An Alternative to Litigation," *The New York Times*, March 4, 1986.

CHAPTER 8

STRATEGIC PLANNING

*S**trategic planning* is concerned with identification and actualization of long-term organizational objectives. This is distinguished from operational planning or the functioning of the organization on a day-to-day basis. In terms of time horizons, it might be helpful to consider that the typical short-range forecast is revised on a quarterly basis and the typical medium-range forecast on an annual basis. Long-range forecasts, in contrast, can project 5 or more years into the future. In fact, some of the most sophisticated organizations such as AT&T, IBM, ITT, and Exxon purportedly work on something in the vicinity of 50-year time lines. But Japan's Matsushita Corporation outdoes these firms, planning strategically some 250 years into the future!

Interestingly, some companies may no longer resemble their former selves at the point of the outer limits of their forecasts. One petrochemical giant, for example, projected that its primary business activity 50 years hence would be space colonization (i.e., providing housing in space). It is easy to understand, therefore, that an inverse relationship exists between the elements of time and accuracy in forecasting. As shown in Figure 8.1, the farther into the future we forecast, the less likely we are to obtain an accurate result.

FIGURE 8.1   THE RELATIONSHIP OF ACCURACY AND TIME IN FORECASTING

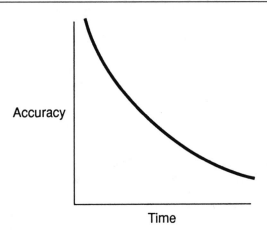

OBJECTIVES, STRATEGIES, AND TACTICS

Business planning is not unlike military planning.[1,2] After all, business involves engaging in warfare, of sorts. And all wars have objectives. Armies fight to win terrain, kill or disable adversary combatants, and/or extract money from their victims. Companies fight to capture market share, generate sales revenues, enhance profits, and/or simply insulate themselves from competition (to the extent that this is possible) by finding a market niche. Both armies and business enterprises try to achieve their objectives through strategies. These "grand" plans are, in turn, transformed into more specific and perhaps more localized measures, commonly known as tactics. Generals and senior executives determine objectives and strategies, whereas field commanders and midlevel executives may have the discretion or authority to determine tactics (i.e., how the strategies are actualized).

A common pitfall in strategic planning pertains to the lack of proper follow-up. I believe that this phenomenon is to some degree justifiably associated with the negative stereotype of the yuppie MBA who is drawn to the perceived glamour of the planning process, yet disdains the formative evaluations and modification or "fine-tuning" of the plans. Clearly, strategic planning must be accompanied by strategic management.

In large organizations, strategic planning is a formalized process and ritual. It invariably leads to creation of a formal written document, the strategic plan. In my conversations with owners of small businesses, I often find that they do not have a formal written document. They typically explain that it's "all in my head." This is unfortunate for three important reasons:

1. *Continuity and succession planning.*

   If the entrepreneur becomes incapacitated or dies, his or her plans for the business die too.

2. *Quality of decisions.*

   Putting ideas to paper actually aids the thought process. In fact, psychologists who subscribe to the "cognitive" psychotherapeutic approach advise their patients to, for example, write down "pro" and "con" considerations concerning a difficult decision in which there may be internal conflict. (If the column of "pro" factors is longer than the column of "con" factors, this might rationally suggest the more appropriate option.)

3. *Commitment.*

   We live in a litigious society, one in which people might be well advised to avoid signing any document (i.e., contract) if it can be avoided. However, if an individual owns and operates a business enterprise, it is reasonable to assume that he or she should be committed to its success. It is in this light that the strategic plan should be viewed as a formal contract entered into with one's self. The written plan serves as a psychological tool to reaffirm this implicit commitment and to strengthen it.

As it would relate to objectives and strategies, growth may be accomplished by:

■ Selling more of the organization's existing products to its current customers;

- Selling new products to existing customers; and/or
- Selling new products to new customers.

The current trend toward globalization can be appreciated better when viewed in the context of growth, for several reasons. First, domestic markets can become exhausted or saturated. Second, the resources required for a large-scale investment may suggest the participation of two or more international or multinational "players" to garner the necessary capital, human, and other resources as well as to share or "pool" the associated risks. And, of course, the increase in quantities bought, produced, and/or sold is often associated with enhanced economies of scale (except in situations involving markets that are too fragmented or too small to be profitable).

However, potential cross-cultural issues must be identified and addressed. A classic example of failure in this regard relates to General Motors' introduction of its popular domestic automobile, the Chevrolet Nova, to the Latin market in South America. The company launched the car there under the same name. Unfortunately for GM, the phrase *no va* in Spanish literally means "does not go." As you might imagine, the results were less than spectacular. A small oversight with serious consequences. The lesson: A little bit of sensitivity to cultural differences can go a long way.

Wouldn't it be nice to have a desk reference that could walk you through the strategic planning process? Well, you'll be pleased to know that Figures 8.2, 8.3, and 8.4 provide "boilerplates" for your convenience;[3] to help you establish your organization's goals, articulate the actions that must be taken to realize these goals and to critique your plan. Explanatory text is provided.

ESTABLISHING CORPORATE OBJECTIVES

1. a. *What is the present condition of the market and our share of it?*

   We must assess the potential growth of the industry and our standing in it.

   b. *Who are the competition and to what extent do they pose a threat?*

   Too often, business strategists not only underestimate the competition, but they sometimes can't even identify who

---

FIGURE 8.2   STEPS IN ESTABLISHING CORPORATE OBJECTIVES

---

1. a. What is the present condition of the market and our share of it?
   b. Who are the competition and to what extent do they pose a risk?
   c. What are our company's strengths and weaknesses?
2. What will our future position be without change?
3. Is this satisfactory?
4. If our future position without change is not satisfactory, what can we do internally to improve things?
5. If our future position without change is not satisfactory, what can we do externally to improve things?
6. What will our future position be if we make these changes?
7. Compare step 2 to step 6.
8. Decide to maintain the status quo or make changes.

FIGURE 8.3   STEPS IN CREATING THE STRATEGIC PLAN

---

1. Analyze the nature of the business.
2. Analyze the macroenvironment.
3. Identify obstacles.
4. Identify opportunities.
5. Determine and quantify goals.
6. Develop plans of action.
7. Determine allocation of finances and other resources.
8. Select methods to measure, review, and control procedures.
9. Submit the proposed written plan for review and approval.

FIGURE 8.4   STEPS IN EVALUATING THE STRATEGIC PLAN

1. Does performance history provide adequate background, or do we need more information?
2. Has the macroenvironment been adequately appraised?
3. Have the capabilities of the organization been thoroughly examined?
4. Have the best opportunities been identified?
5. Have all opportunities and downside risks been identified?
6. Have all possible alternative strategies been considered?
7. Does the marketing mix flow logically from the chosen strategy?
8. Are recommended projects necessary and properly funded?
9. Are financial data clear and consistent?
10. Have benchmarks and controls been established?
11. Is the strategic plan compatible with prevailing attitudes, interests and opinions (i.e., corporate culture, public image)?
12. Is the strategic plan defensible?

---

the competition really is. Showtime, the cable entertainment programming company, realized that it wasn't just competing against other premium cable services, such as HBO. In fact, it was competing against home video rental companies. Research discovered that many cable TV subscribers were discontinuing service because they perceived a relative advantage with video rentals. After all, videos enable the customer to view a movie of one's choice at a time convenient to the customer, whereas cable TV programs or movies are transmitted on a fixed schedule which may not be convenient. Moreover, cable TV programming schedules varied from day to day, complicated further by the perception that some published guides or schedule lists were difficult to read. How did Showtime respond? The company launched a campaign that involved showing a feature every evening at a fixed time, implicitly inviting subscribers to videotape the movies.

c. *What are our company's strengths and weaknesses?*

Simply put, this is the decision maker's moment of truth. This is the time to assess what is, not what he or she would like it to be. An accurate assessment here is absolutely necessary to set realistic objectives. There may be a natural tendency to focus on maximizing strengths while paying less attention to weaknesses. It is human nature to gravitate toward that which "feels good" rather than that which does not. Paradoxically, though, facing up to weaknesses and redoubling efforts to address them is, in our business lives as well as in our personal lives, a sign of strength.

2. *What will our future position be without change?*

(See "Forecasting Methods" later in this chapter.)

3. *Is this satisfactory?*

"Change" can be a very touchy subject. Too often, good decisions are rejected in favor of the status quo or those that are "comfortable." Clearly, comfortable is not necessarily best.

4. *If our future position without change is not satisfactory, what can we do **internally** to improve things?*

We might, for example, alter our modus operandi in the areas of marketing, research and development, human resources, facilities, and equipment.

5. *If we view our future position without change as unsatisfactory, what can we do **externally** to improve things?*

We might, for example, evaluate the feasibility of entering different, new industries or fields and perhaps even acquiring existing companies toward that end. In any event, we would establish criteria in terms of demonstrated or anticipated levels of sales, profitability, and rate of growth. We would also evaluate the extent to which the move allows us to take advantage of synergies. In other words, does the opportunity (or company to be acquired) "fit" and help to make "the whole greater than the sum of its parts"? And, of course, we must assess whether we have the managerial competence and financial resources to make for success.

6. *What will our future position be if we make these changes?*

7. *Compare step 2 to step 6.*

8. *Decide to "stay the course" or make changes.*

Creating the Strategic Plan

1. *Analyze the nature of the business.* (By the way, what business is the company really in?)

   When we think of General Motors, for example, we perceive that GM is primarily in the business of manufacturing automobiles. However, the company earns more from its financing division, General Motors Acceptance Corporation (GMAC), than it does from its manufacturing operations. Similarly, the publishers of *TV Guide* (the weekly television viewer's magazine) enjoy a higher market valuation (i.e., stock price) than do any of the TV networks. So perhaps the more appropriate question should be: "What business should the company really be in?"[4]

   William Wrigley apparently knew the correct answer. A century ago, he was in the baking powder business. As an incentive to buy his product, Wrigley offered customers two free packs of chewing gum with each purchase. This gambit to "double their pleasure" proved so successful that he left the baking powder business entirely and built a chewing gum empire that nets approximately $2 billion a year.

   Too often, there is a tendency to narrow rather than broaden an organization's self-image—and this has the effect of limiting its potential opportunities. So, if an organization views itself as being in the motion picture business (i.e., narrow), it might be healthier to view itself as being in the entertainment business or, better yet, the communication business.

In any event, the organization must have a clearly defined *raison d'être* or purpose. This should be conveyed in a brief *mission statement* that expresses the company's ultimate goal. It generally emerges from discussions and exercises geared toward corporate soul-searching or introspection and reflects the organization's values. The mission statement also addresses the company's ability to differentiate itself from the competition; to be unique and special. Antonio Stradivari, the craftsman of what is widely regarded as the world's finest violin (the Stradivarius), expressed his philosophy and sense of purpose 300 years ago in his version of a mission statement: "God needs violins to send His music into the world, and if any violins are defective God's music will be spoiled. Other men will make other violins, but no man shall make a better one."

2. *Analyze the macroenvironment.*

Factor the exogenous or uncontrollable variables that impact on your business. These include sociocultural, politicolegal, technoscientific, economic, and competitive factors (see "The Macroenvironment" in Chapter 1).

3. *Identify opportunities.*

4. *Identify obstacles.*

Sometimes decision makers "can't see the forest for the trees." They are too close to a decision area to be objective or simply imaginative. For this reason, it might be wise to bring in an "outsider," an external consultant or merely a peer who does not have a vested interest or preconceived notion.

Early in the 1980s, Time, Incorporated, launched *TV-Cable Week* magazine. Senior managers purportedly assumed that since the corporation owned American Television and Communications (ATC), the second largest cable system operator, as well as Home Box Office (HBO), the largest program supplier, a cable TV guide would be a great success. So they thought: "Why bother to conduct a market test?" (It should be noted that Time's decision makers chose this course of action even though ATC management had reservations about the project early on.) Moreover, the two Harvard MBAs employed by Time and assigned to forecast the future performance of the prospective new publication tempered their optimistic projections with the recommendation that testing would be prudent and appropriate. The result: the vast majority of cable system operators (including Time's own ATC) had no interest in *TV-Cable Week* and the magazine soon folded its operation. This episode is widely regarded as one of the most expensive and fascinating debacles in the history of print media. It illustrates how the arrogance of senior management can cause an organization to suffer substantial cash losses and far greater losses in the market value of its stock.[5]

5. *Determine and quantify goals.*

There are, of course, different types of goals. Some organizations want to be the leaders in their industries as measured in sales revenues, while others focus on profitability as measured in return on investment. Other firms strive primarily to insulate themselves from competition, under the premise that their market "niche" will ensure their survival if not their growth and prosperity. In fact, there are even a few companies that place a premium on organizational "quality of life," such that growth is actually unwelcome. Yvon Chouinard, the iconoclastic owner of Patagonia, which manufactures high-ticket outdoor apparel, has actually said "I just don't want to get any bigger."[6]

All objectives must be quantifiable, expressed in magnitude: market share as a percentage, sales volume in absolute dollars, and so on. Time frames or benchmarks for realizing objectives (and each stage thereof) must also be stated specifically. Naturally, it is necessary that the implementing team responsible for reaching the objectives be identified as well, with each member's role clearly defined.

6. *Develop plans of action.*

Create the strategies and tactics that will be employed to realize the objectives. It is essential that these plans be logical and achievable (i.e., realistic). They must also be congruent with organizational culture. For example, the Disney organization assessed its future and realized that its prospects for growth were limited by

its exclusive commitment to wholesome, family-oriented entertainment. Research indicated that motion pictures with adult
themes (i.e., those likely to receive "R" ratings), which might involve nudity and objectionable language, would fare well at the
box office and for Disney, too. But this new direction would
hardly be "congruent" with the Disney image and culture. So,
what did the company do? Disney formed Touchstone, a subsidiary, to make motion pictures for the adult audience, and the
Disney reputation was not the least bit sullied.

7. *Determine allocation of finances and other resources.*

The name of the game is "budget." In terms of organizational finance, it is better to control more money than you need than not
enough. In some organizations, you would be permitted to use
the "excess" money for purposes other than those that were originally approved, whereas in other organizations, internal accounting rules would require you to give back money that is not used
for the purposes specifically intended. In terms of corporate poli-
tics, the more budget or money you control, the greater your potential for power within the organization.

8. *Select methods to measure, review, and control procedures.*

The term *variance analysis* pertains to the difference between what
we plan or anticipate and what actually occurs. If we are pleased
with the result, we may stay the course or step up our activities. If
we are not pleased, we may make adjustments in the plan or the
way the plan is executed.

9. *Submit the proposed written plan for review and approval.*

In business as well as military organizations, the best of strategic
plans are substantively influenced by the divisional or depart-
mental reports submitted by subordinates to those more senior
decision makers who actually formulate and "sign off" on the
plans. In other words, a manager may have more influence than
he or she may realize. Management theory as well as practice tend
to support the contention that the most well-run and profitable organizations are those in which influence can flow upward

through the organizational hierarchy, such that the entity can be said to be managed "bottom up."

EVALUATING THE STRATEGIC PLAN

Given the importance of the document, it would be wise to give the strategic plan the benefit of a sober critique. A checklist is provided in Figure 8.4. In addition, it wouldn't hurt to have a third party (such as impartial colleagues or even external consultants) play "devil's advocate" and try to poke holes in the plan. If they can pierce the armor of your document, then clearly, there is more work ahead of you. If they cannot, then you can proceed with confidence. Either way, you win.

FORECASTING METHODS

We discussed quantitative methods in Chapter 4, or statistics. Let us now address qualitative methods. These deal with "what people do" and "what people say" and are viewed as "soft," subjective, and vulnerable to challenge.

When I was studying for my MBA, one assignment that I will always remember involved the study of forecasting methods within a major corporation of my choice. A requirement of the assignment was that I personally interview a senior executive involved in the planning function. As it happened, I chose Clairol and found myself sitting with a senior vice president. He lit a cigar, leaned back in his chair in anticipation of my questions, and said, "Shoot, kid." My first question asked him to identify the quantitative forecasting methods he relied upon. He asked what I meant by "quantitative." I suggested regression analysis and some other number-crunching methods, to kick things off. "I don't use 'em," he responded. "What, then, do you use?" I asked. He leaned forward, savoring the moment with this "green" student, and said with a smile, "I ask my sales managers what they think." (See "Sales Force Estimates" later on the next page.)

Based upon my own empirical information and the anecdotes of my fellow management consultants, I can only say that most people would be very surprised to know just how many "sophisticated" organizations rely so heavily on "soft" or qualitative methods.

Qualitative Methods

The following methods are among the most commonly used:

Executive Judgment

Based on the input of top management, this method relies on the team's experience, talents, and instincts. While it can be valuable if management's track record is good, it sometimes reflects an "ivory tower" perspective when these individuals insulate themselves from what is really going on among rank-and-file employees and customers. The less time that management spends in the executive suites and the more time that it devotes to keeping current and close to employees and customers, the less the danger that this approach poses.

Expert Opinion

Based on the expertise of external consultants, this method can bring highly specialized and valuable assistance to the table. However, management may retain such consultants to provide a "rubber stamp" or approval for actions that had already been taken and may go bad.

Sales Force Estimates

This source of input can be of great value, since the salesperson is generally closest to the customer. This is of particular importance within technologically volatile industries. The primary danger lies in the potential for bias, since salespeople may believe that their estimates will be used to establish quotas to which they will have to adhere.

Consumer Surveys and Market Tests

Consumer surveys involve gathering information directly from the consumer, using market research techniques. An example that comes to mind is the Pepsi "taste test," which involved asking consumers to sample Pepsi-Cola and Coca-Cola and to indicate their preference. However, findings can be very inaccurate if sampling is not representative (see Chapter 4 on statistics) or if questionnaire design is flawed. Supposedly,

Coca-Cola's decision to withdraw the "old Coke" from distribution a decade ago is attributable in part to imprecise phrasing of a survey question. The question did not specifically ask how the consumer would feel about the prospect of Coke being taken off the market.

Market tests involve promotion and distribution of a brand on a limited basis. Generally, new brands are tested in "bellwether" markets, those key cities or towns that are representative of the consumer universe. Ostensibly, if the brand does well in these markets, it may "launch" or "roll out" on a national basis. However, if product weaknesses are detected, the brand may need to be improved or perhaps even abandoned. A risk inherent in conducting market tests is that they can be monitored by competitors. Remember that these corporate "spies" can gain valuable information from your efforts.

Group Discussion

This is decision by committee or consensus. All members of the group must agree on a single decision (i.e., come up with "a number they can live with"). When it works, the method is usually indicative of group cohesiveness. However, a "bully" may exert undue influence on the other members of the group to get them to agree with him.

The motion picture *Twelve Angry Men* illustrates this point rather well. The story involves a jury brought together to decide the guilt or innocence of a young man charged with manslaughter. A juror initially succeeds in pressuring all but one of his fellow jurors into agreeing with his guilty vote. The single "holdout" juror stands up to the bully and, ultimately, the entire jury votes to acquit the defendant.

Pooled Individual

Individual estimates are merged, and an average is derived. Each person's estimate has equal weight. Therefore, this method may be regarded as "democratic."

Delphi

In this variant of pooled individual, participants submit their individual estimates and then review those of other participants. They may then discuss and revise their original figures. In this sense, it may be regarded as a hybrid version of group discussion and pooled individual, drawing upon the strengths of each approach.

Quali-Quant Methods

As you can see, much decision making is based upon unknown factors and often upon subjective estimates. It is only natural, therefore, to seek out and apply some sort of "scientific method" in these "soft" situations, to make the process as objective as possible. Toward that end, we may elect to use Bayesian methods to provide us with the semblance of a quantitative formula to make qualitative and subjective (i.e., "soft") inputs "harder."

Index of Attractiveness

The index of attractiveness enables us to rank projects or products in order of their projected profitability. If funds are limited, the index can be used to help determine which ones to drop from consideration.

To calculate the index of attractiveness, we multiply the value representing its probability of successful development (T, expressed as a percentage) by the value representing its probability of commercial success if it is actually brought to market (C, expressed as a percentage). The resulting figure is multiplied by the value representing the amount of profit that is expected to be generated in the event of commercial success (P, expressed in absolute dollars). The total is then divided by the value representing the cost of development (D, expressed in absolute dollars).

The formula for the index of attractiveness is presented in Figure 8.5.

Decision Making Under Uncertainty: The Payoff Matrix

This formula enables us to estimate the payoffs associated with various scenarios and strategies and ultimately to choose the strategy that is likely to give us the best payoff.[7] (The implication here is that we may have to commit to a particular single strategy before we can determine which scenario will actually occur.) To identify the best strategy, we multiply each scenario's chance of occurring by the payoff (e.g., profit) associated with each strategy option for each of the scenarios. We then add up

| | FIGURE 8.5 | CALCULATING THE INDEX OF ATTRACTIVENESS |

The formula for the index of attractiveness is:

$$\frac{T \times C \times P}{D} = \text{Index of attractiveness rating}$$

where

T = probability of successful development
C = probability of commerical success
P = profit, if successful
D = cost of development

Using this formula, we compute ratings for the four projects as follows:

Project	T (%)	× C (%)	× P ($)	/ D ($)	= Rating
A	0.8	0.6	5,000,000	200,000 =	12.00
B	0.6	0.9	1,000,000	500,000 =	1.08
C	0.6	0.8	10,000,000	700,000 =	8.00
D	0.9	0.7	11,000,000	3,000,000 =	2.31

The higher the rating, the more attractive the option is likely to be. Therefore, we would rank the projects as follows:

1. Project A (12.00)
2. Project C (8.00)
3. Project D (2.31)
4. Project B (1.08)

Note: The values for the variables T, C, P, and D are subjective estimates (derived by any of the qualitative forecasting methods, for example). Index of attractiveness is a "quali-quant" method because those subjective estimates (qualitative input) are manipulated by a formula (quantitative framework).

the subtotals for each strategy option and select the strategy option with highest payoff (see Figure 8.6).

Decision Making Under Conflict: Game Theory

Developed by legendary mathematician John von Neumann, this approach is similar to decision making under uncertainty. However, it explicitly factors in the notion that our adversaries make rational decisions and take actions in response to our own actions.[8] In other words, decision making and business game playing don't exist in a vacuum; your adversaries are plotting their chess moves against you just as you move against them.

Decision Tree

This tool allows us to depict visually possible scenarios (i.e., branches on the tree) that may spawn even more scenarios (i.e., subsequent scenarios or smaller branches on the tree).[9]

FIGURE 8.6   DECISION MAKING UNDER UNCERTAINTY

Note: The values or numbers depicted here represent subjective estimates and were chosen arbitrarily for illustrative purposes only.

The formula for ranking strategy options using decision making under uncertainty is:

$$CP \text{ for } A = (PSN \times IP) + (PSN \times IP) + (PSN \times IP) + \cdots$$

where

A = each strategy option
SN = each scenario
IP = payoff for each strategy under each scenario set
CP = payoff for each strategy under all scenario sets

FIGURE 8.6 *(Continued)*

We are asked to assume that scenario 1 (SN_1) has a 40 percent chance of occurring, scenario 2 (SN_2) has a 20 percent chance of occurring, scenario 3 (SN_3) has a 15 percent chance of occurring, and scenario 4 (SN_4) has a 25 percent chance of occurring. We may choose any one of three alternative strategies (A_1, A_2, or A_3). The numbers inside the accompanying matrix represent the payoff associated with each strategy for each scenario. Figures in brackets show how payoffs are computed.

	SN_1 (0.40)	SN_2 (0.20)	SN_3 (0.15)	SN_4 (0.25)	= Payoff
A_1	9	3	5	6	= 6.45
	[(0.40 × 9) + (0.20 × 3) + (0.15 × 5) + (0.25 × 6)]				
A_2	6	5	7	4	= 5.45
	[(0.40 × 6) + (0.20 × 5) + (0.15 × 7) + (0.25 × 4)]				
A_3	4	8	4	8	= 5.80
	[(0.40 × 4) + (0.20 × 8) + (0.15 × 4) + (0.25 × 8)]				

Let's assume further, in terms of the weather, that

SN_1 = it will rain
SN_2 = it will snow
SN_3 = it will be warm and humid
SN_4 = it will be clear and dry

FIGURE 8.7 *(Continued)*

and that

A_1 = carry an umbrella
A_2 = wear a winter coat
A_3 = wear a T-shirt and shorts

So, given that strategy A_1 offers the highest payoff, we would carry an umbrella in anticipation of rain.

Note: In the "real world," planning exists on more than a single plane and is multidimensional and often very complex. To consider dozens or even hundreds of alternative strategies in the face of a similar number of scenarios would not be unrealistic.

Figure 8.7 depicts the four "primary" scenarios corresponding to Figure 8.6. It goes on to suggest secondary or subsequent scenarios. For example, SN_1 branches off into two resulting scenarios, each of which has a 50 percent chance of occurring. The probability of either occurring would be 20 percent ($0.40 \times 0.50 = 0.20$).

The Aggregate or Merged Forecast

If you are using more than one forecasting method, how do you come up with a single "bottom-line" forecast? This is accomplished by multiplying the forecast amount or input for each method by a weighting percentage reflecting the degree to which we are willing to rely upon that method. We then add the subtotals to derive a single forecast figure.

FIGURE 8.7   DECISION TREE

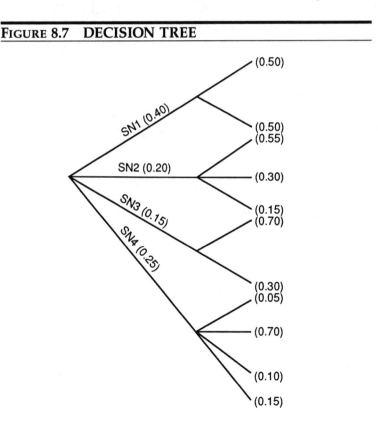

Figure 8.8 shows the merging of four different forecasting methods we have discussed earlier. (Of course, you could decide to use other or additional methods, including quantitative approaches such as regression analysis; see Chapter 4 on statistics.) In this example, the results of executive judgment, expert opinion, sales force estimates, and customer surveys are multiplied by the weighting percentage (an expression of how reliable we think each forecast is likely to be). This percentage may reflect how reliable a method has been in the past or how reliable we believe it will be based upon a new development. In any case, the percentages for all methods that are used must add up to 100 percent. By adding together these four subtotals, we get the aggregate projection.

Let us assume that we find, at the end of the year, that the forecast in this example was pretty much "right on the money" and that sales revenues were actually very close to the $10 million figure. We would then assign greater weighting to executive judgment in next year's forecast, perhaps allowing it a weighting of 50 or so percent and adjusting the weightings for the other methods accordingly.

As you can see, strategic planning is a very broad functional area spanning the range of business disciplines. It involves the identification of organizational objectives and the translation of these into strategies that, in turn, are implemented as tactical or "action" plans, for day-to-day

---

FIGURE 8.8   AGGREGATE OR MERGED FORECAST

Combine or merge the results of various forecasting methods so that each can be "weighted" and be a component of the overall projection.

Method	Forecast Amount (millions)	Weighting	Input (millions)
Executive judgment	$10	0.30	$ 3
Expert opinion	8	0.25	2
Sales force estimates	20	0.20	4
Customer survey	4	0.25	1
		1.00	

Aggregate projection: $10 million

operational activities. More than any other area, strategic planning calls for the integration of countervailing qualities and considerations: creative and analytical, long term and short term; strengths and weaknesses; opportunities and threats.

THE STRATEGIC PLANNING CHECKLIST

1. Are my corporate objectives realistic and appropriate?
2. Is the strategic plan likely to help realize these objectives?
3. How can I critique and refine it?
4. Have I been completely honest with myself in assessing the organization's strengths and weaknesses?
5. In what ways can I improve my forecasting?
6. Who in my organization will be involved in these functions?

RECOMMENDED READING

Aaker, David, *Developing Business Strategies* (New York: John Wiley and Sons, 1984).

Ascher, William, *Strategic Planning and Forecasting* (New York: John Wiley and Sons, 1983).

Melcher, Bonita H., *Strategic Planning* (New York: TAB Books, 1988).

Rue, Leslie W., *Strategic Management* (New York: McGraw-Hill, 1986).

Stahl, Michael J., *Strategic Executive Decisions* (New York: Quorum Books, 1989).

ORGANIZATIONS AND RESOURCES

International Association of Business Forecasting
1587 Town Hill Road
York Springs, PA 17372
(312) 508-2291

International Association of Business Strategy Consultants
P.O. Box 5219
Akron, OH 44313
(216) 836-4410

ENDNOTES

1. David J. Rogers, *Waging Business Warfare* (New York: Kensington, 1987).

2. John McDonald, *Strategy in Poker, Business & War* (New York: W. W. Norton, 1989).

3. Format suggested by I. Robert Parket.

4. Stan Davis and Bill Davidson, *2020 Vision* (New York: Simon & Schuster, 1991).

5. Christopher M. Byron, *The Fanciest Dive* (New York: W. W. Norton, 1983)

6. Andrew E. Serwer, "Patagonia CEO Reels Company In," *Fortune*, December 14, 1992.

7. Hamdy A. Taha, *Operations Research* (New York: Macmillan, 1976).

8. Stephen D. Casler, *Introduction to Economics* (New York: HarperCollins, 1992).

9. Taha, *Operations Research*.

CHAPTER 9

EDUCATION AND CAREER PATHING

YOU ARE A PRODUCT!

In planning your career objectives and the educational means likely to
help you actualize them, you might find it helpful to employ a multidisciplinary approach similar to the one that MBAs use in making business
decisions (given a little creative license, of course). Toward that end, ponder these points:

Marketing

In seeking a job, the blunt truth is that *you are a product*. It is important that you differentiate your brand (i.e., yourself) from other brands
competing against you in the marketplace (i.e., other job seekers). So it is
important that you identify and evaluate the sets of skills and educational accomplishments that will best help you differentiate and position
your product. For example, you might choose to enter a joint JD/MBA
program, garnering a law degree as well as a business degree. Or you

might pursue a major in telephony (i.e., telephone, radio, and satellite communications), a very hot area of expertise. Or you might learn a foreign language or two (conversationally, if not fluently). True story: As I was winding down a recent MBA IN A NUTSHELL® class and welcoming questions, a student asked my advice regarding how he, a computer systems analyst who speaks five European languages fluently, might find a job. Before I could answer, another student (who just happened to manage international operations in her organization) addressed her peer with two sweet-sounding words: "You're hired."

Accounting and Finance

Assess your net worth (in the career universe), identifying and ascribing values of magnitude to your assets and weaknesses. Weigh educational options not only in terms of their potential to increase your net worth, but also in terms of their NPV, IRR, and ROI. In other words, you would want to estimate the probable payoff or value of the time and money that you may invest in your development.

Economics

In terms of diminishing marginal utility, ascertain just "how much (education) is enough." Also, consider what the demand for your product is now and is likely to be in the future.

Statistics

Get your hands on a lot of research (the secondary or preexisting kind will do just fine). Get the information to support your preliminary decisions. Look for relationships and trends.

Human Resources Management

Use a Myers-Briggs Type Inventory® or some other tool to help you reach valuable insights about your personality characteristics and the implications these have in terms of the nature of job tasks, work settings, as well as types of learning that would suit you the best. Also, create some-thing akin to an MBO to help you commit to actualizing specific educa-tional and/or career goals within particular time frames.

Off the record, I can't begin to tell you how many "successful" peo-ple I meet who are very unhappy in their careers. One that immediately comes to mind: the highly paid corporate executive who started out as a schoolteacher but was pressured to study for an MBA and get on the fast track, because his family told him that he "should" earn more money. He confided in me that the financial rewards he receives in the business world pale when compared to the gratification he got from helping kids develop in their formative years. To live your life according to the expec-tations of others rather than realizing your *raison d'être* is such a tragic waste. In the words of Joseph Campbell, "Follow your bliss. The money will come." And I say that if it doesn't come, that's not so bad. You're still better off.

Strategic Planning

Weigh all the aforementioned points and integrate your assessments in a strategic plan. Chart your course. The following self-diagnostic tool (Figure 9.1) may be helpful toward that end.

DO YOU REALLY NEED AN MBA?

That depends upon the following considerations:

Career Stage and Aspirations

Where are you now in the hierarchy of your organization? How well do you know your industry? Are you a seasoned veteran or a relative newcomer? Generally, the MBA credential can at best only allow you ac-cess to the so-called "fast track." It does not guarantee that you will as-cend to the dizzying heights of the executive suite. On balance, if you are a "shirt-sleeves" manager who has received promotions at regular inter-vals and are otherwise pleased with your progress, pursuit of the MBA

FIGURE 9.1   CAREER SELF-EXAMINATION

Directions: Place a square around a number to indicate how important you feel that item is to your career position. Place a circle around a number to indicate what you perceive your present situation to be.

Scale: High/Excellent — 5 — 4 — 3 — 2 — 1 — Low/Poor

Items:

1. Making as much money as is normal for your job in other organizations.   5 4 3 2 1

2. Making as much money as you need.   5 4 3 2 1

3. Making as much money as you want.   5 4 3 2 1

4. Having the opportunity to increase your income significantly while in this firm.   5 4 3 2 1

5. Having vertical growth opportunities in the organization (upward in management).   5 4 3 2 1

6. Having lateral growth opportunities in the organization (other jobs or career paths).   5 4 3 2 1

7. Living in the part of the country where you want to live.   5 4 3 2 1

8. Living locally where you want to live.   5 4 3 2 1

9. Having satisfactory time/energy balance between job and personal life.   5 4 3 2 1

10. Having job security.   5 4 3 2 1

11. Having your family/significant others satisfied with your career path choice.   5 4 3 2 1

12. Having your family/significant others satisfied with your present job.   5 4 3 2 1

13. Being generally satisfied with this organization.   5 4 3 2 1

14. Having the opportunity to be creative in this organization.   5 4 3 2 1

15. Having a reasonable work schedule.   5 4 3 2 1

16. Having a satisfactory work environment.   5 4 3 2 1

FIGURE 9.1   *(Continued)*

---

17. Having opportunities to update/learn new
    skills.   5 4 3 2 1

18. Taking pride in your job.   5 4 3 2 1

19. Having opportunities for career path
    counseling.   5 4 3 2 1

20. Taking pride in the organization.   5 4 3 2 1

21. Being satisfied with your coworkers.   5 4 3 2 1

22. Being satisfied with your supervisor/manager.   5 4 3 2 1

23. Being satisfied with upper management.   5 4 3 2 1

24. Avoiding excessive job stress and burnout.   5 4 3 2 1

25. Making a positive contribution to the
    organization.   5 4 3 2 1

Your present overall career satisfaction:

Scale: (circle one)

Very High—10—9—8—7—6—5—4—3—2—1—Very Low

Taking into account your present career situation—age,
experience, skills, talents, contacts, and so forth—what do you
think your job satisfaction could be?

                                  10 9 8 7 6 5 4 3 2 1

If there is a significant difference between your present career
satisfaction and what you think it could be, what might you
need to narrow the gap?

What might you need to do to lessen any significant differences
between the squares and the circles—the importance and the
current position—in your self-assessment?

Source: John Douglas Stewart, *The Power of People Skills* (Wiley and Sons, Copyrighted 1986) pp. 208–209. Reprinted in 1993 by University Press of America.

would probably not offer much utility, unless you are on a periphery of senior management or already within its ranks. In that case, having or not having the degree might make the difference between being considered for a particular slot or not.

Corporate Culture and Personal Orientation

Does your employer (or the norms of your industry or specific job function) implicitly or explicitly require the credential? In many instances, employers would prefer to hire bright and eager individuals with baccalaureates in any number of academic areas and train them in the company's own way. As a matter of fact, none other than the respected Procter & Gamble operates in this manner, to the extent that even MBAs who are hired out of business schools purportedly must put in time stocking supermarket shelves and performing some of the less glamorous tasks not usually associated with the patina of the MBA. Clearly, the emphasis in such an environment, at least at the beginning of one's career, is learning the business "from the bottom up." And that may cause some dirt to accumulate under the fingernails.

Of course, if you are an entrepreneur and "career track" as such is not an issue, the credential may hold little value. The value of the body of knowledge associated with the credential is, of course, considerable. Yet it is possible to acquire it (or the components of it that you actually need) through other courses of action. (By the way, many entrepreneurs already do on a daily basis and take for granted what MBA candidates learn about in their lessons and case studies. In fact, I have even met a number of successful entrepreneurs who intuitively know what MBAs strive to learn.)

Time Constraints

Do your job schedule and personal commitments allow you to devote time to class attendance, homework assignments, and study? Keep in mind that the typical full-time (i.e., daytime) MBA program requires two years, while the degree may be attained in three to five years of part-time (i.e., evening) study or three consecutive full-time (i.e., daytime) summer sessions over three years.

Some universities have established "Executive MBA" programs specially suited to fast-track corporate executives and successful entrepreneurs. Admission (for other than entrepreneurs) often requires employer sponsorship, and for this reason, candidates tend to be the "fair-haired boys and girls" rather than rank-and-file aspiring executives. To accommodate the student's business obligations, the course of study may involve one full day per week of class attendance during the academic year, along with a three-week intensive summer session over a two-year period.

Some organizations make only a "lip service" commitment to learning opportunities and development of its employees, while others such as IBM, make a very serious commitment. In fact, IBM's executive new hires are purportedly required to attend several weeks of training before they even report to the office. There is a distinction, however, between "training" on the company's time and "education" on or off the company's time.

Cost

Are you prepared to spend $20,000 to $35,000 for tuition or is your employer (or other third party) prepared to foot the bill? As with time constraints, corporate culture is another key deciding factor.

CHOOSING AN MBA PROGRAM

If you have decided that getting an MBA will empower you to achieve your career goals, the following considerations should be weighed in selecting the program best suited to your needs:

The Institution

Is the school properly accredited? This is generally an important criterion. To what extent is the school's curriculum geared to a specific industry? If you are committed to a career in the insurance field, for example, an MBA granted by the College of Insurance might make a lot of sense, whereas it might not if you are contemplating a career other than insurance.

The Department

What percentage of the faculty is retained on a full-time rather than part-time (i.e., adjunct) basis? What percentage have earned doctorates? What percentage publish scholarly articles and are involved in formal research projects? The answers to these questions tend to illustrate the extent to which the department is geared toward scholarship.

The Learning Environment

Are classes small and individualized, or are students "warehoused" in huge lecture halls? Perhaps a particular blend of the two settings would best accommodate your particular learning style. Are the library and computer facilities extensive and "state of the art"? They should be.

Employment Search Support

Does the job placement office have a strong track record in arranging interviews with better firms, or is it pretty much a waste of time? Does the alumni club function as an "old boys/girls network," helping to place graduates by drawing upon its membership resources? Clearly, the greater the support, the better (assuming, of course, that you place a premium on having it).

ALTERNATIVES TO THE MBA

In the wake of the 1987 stock market crash and on the heels of a subsequent recession, the value of the MBA credential has been called into question by some human resources executives, educators, and graduate business school students and their "would-be" counterparts who wonder whether the course of study is still worth the effort. Taking into consideration the limitations of the aspiring learner, the following options are offered as viable alternatives to the traditional MBA course of study:

Other Graduate Programs and Degrees

As the saying goes, there is more than one way to skin a cat. Study in the fields of natural science and technology as well as behavioral science also present significant potential springboards.

Applications in Science and Technology

M.S.T.M.	Master of Science in Technology Management
M.S.E.E.	Master of Science in Electrical Engineering
M.S.Ch.E.	Master of Science in Chemical Engineering
M.S.I.E.	Master of Science in Industrial Engineering
M.S.M.E.	Master of Science in Mechanical Engineering

Applications in Human Resources Management

M.S.I.L.R.	Master of Science in Industrial Labor Relations
M.S.Ed.	Master of Science in Education

Applications in International/Cross-cultural Spheres

M.S.I.A.	Master of Science in International Affairs

Certificate Programs

Universities also offer education modules of shorter duration and of a more specialized nature. In a mere four to ten days, an individual may participate in a certificate-granting program specializing in advanced sales management, corporate finance, human resources management, operations research, telecommunications management, strategic planning, or any of hundreds of other offerings that may deal in areas of subspecialization (i.e., compensation or industrial labor relations rather than the general discipline of human resources management). I am a big fan of certificate programs, and I have found that job interviewers often tend to value a certificate granted by a prestigious school over the MBA credential granted by anything less than a top business school. This is especially true when interviewing seasoned managers rather than those at or near entry level. Moreover, the opportunity to "network" with peers during and after these programs can be rich. The price tag ranges from approximately $3,000 to $8,000.

Synoptic or MBA Overview Programs

Private management consulting firms and corporate training organizations may offer "overviews" of the MBA curriculum. The seminar is of a highly intensive nature, ranging from two to five full days in duration, designed to present the essence of the MBA body of knowledge in just a few days. The range of quality within this category is broad. One program may be delivered by a university professor who, despite respectable academic credentials, refers primarily to "textbook" points of reference and views the business community from an "ivory tower" of sorts. Another program delivered by an educator with a background in management consulting or corporate training and similarly impressive credentials (i.e., a doctorate and professional recognition) may focus to a greater extent on the "real-world" perspective of business. The price tag is generally $700 to $3,500. (The author's popular MBA IN A NUTSHELL is delivered worldwide: tuition is approximately $695 per person. Corporate seminars for 30 or more participants (for a moderate flat fee) can be arranged. For more information, Dr. Sobel invites you to contact him via fax (212) 684-4329 or e-mail: drsobel@tiac.net)

To the extent that we regard the MBA curriculum (if not the credential) as a legitimate vehicle for professional and perhaps personal growth, it is my contention that we are living in times that warrant considerable optimism. The elitist stigma of the MBA and the "yuppie" image with which it is sometimes associated are things of the past. I suggest that virtually anyone who wants to learn what an MBA is expected to know can do so, inexpensively and within a relatively short amount of time. This is the era of "Everyman's MBA." Find the version that feels right for your purposes. It's out there. Study.

RECOMMENDED READING

Jones, Constance, *Beat the MBAs to the Top!* (Reading MA: Addison-Wesley, 1987).

Hawes, Gene R., *The College Board Guide to Going to College While Working* (Princeton, NJ: The College Board, 1990).

Kurst, Charlette, (ed.), *The Official Guide to MBA Programs* (New York: Warner Books, 1990).

Bard, Ray, and Susan K. Elliot, *The National Directory of Corporate Training Programs* (New York: Stonesong/Doubleday, 1988).

Salzman, Marian, and Nancy Marx, *MBA Jobs!* (New York: AMA-COM, 1986).

ORGANIZATIONS AND RESOURCES

Graduate Management Admissions Council
11601 Wilshire Blvd., 10th Floor
Los Angeles, CA 90025
(213) 478-1433

Dr. Milo Sobel
The Coronet Consulting Group*
7 Park Avenue, Suite 20-B
New York, New York 10016
(212) 684-4622

*This company is owned by the author. If you wish to attend the MBA IN A NUTSHELL® seminar or obtain any of Dr. Sobel's other educational materials, he welcomes your inquiry.

EPILOGUE: REFLECTION, INTROSPECTION, AND ENLIGHTENMENT

MANAGEMENT DECISION MAKING: ART OR SCIENCE?

As we near completion of *The 12-Hour MBA Program,* you might be wondering: Is management decision making an art or a science?

Algorithms and Heuristics

Clearly, there are scientific methods and bodies of knowledge that can be of great value to managers. Yet, especially in today's complex business environment, many situations do not easily lend themselves to problem solving by means of algorithms, the formulas or equations used to solve problems with virtually assured accuracy. Instead, managers are often forced to rely on their sets of heuristics, their value-laden assumptions or "rules of thumb."

I remember that when I rented my first apartment, the widely accepted heuristic of the day dictated that individuals should not spend more than one quarter of their monthly take-home pay on rent. As the cost of housing has risen over the years, very few people in my city find that they can abide by this heuristic. So the problem with heuristics is that they can become obsolete with the passage of time—and managers may not realize that the heuristics that may have served them well in the past have become obsolete.

Can you identify or characterize some of the heuristics that you depend upon?

Might other heuristics, upon reflection, serve you better?

The illustration in Figure 1 depicts the face of a telephone. This is what you see when you use the instrument. You will notice that the 12 buttons you would press to dial a telephone number are left blank. Fill them in, with the correct numbers, letters, and/or special characters and symbols. (Do not read further until you have completed this exercise.)

Change: The Cognitive and the Affective

Management decision making involves not only how we think (i.e., the cognitive), but also how we feel (i.e., the affective). And one of the most pressing issues in business today is how we feel about change. Change is inevitable and unavoidable. So do we anticipate it and embrace it or do we fight it? Too often, we fight it. This may be attributed to any of the following:

- We may not understand the nature of a particular change. For example, an individual who does not understand computer technology might reasonably resist it.
- We may fear that introduction of a particular change will cause us to lose power within the organization; and
- We may have "plateaued" and no longer wish to assume a new challenge.

  To what extent do you resist change?

  How do you feel about that?

  How do you feel about how you feel?

FIGURE 1   MEMORY EXERCISE

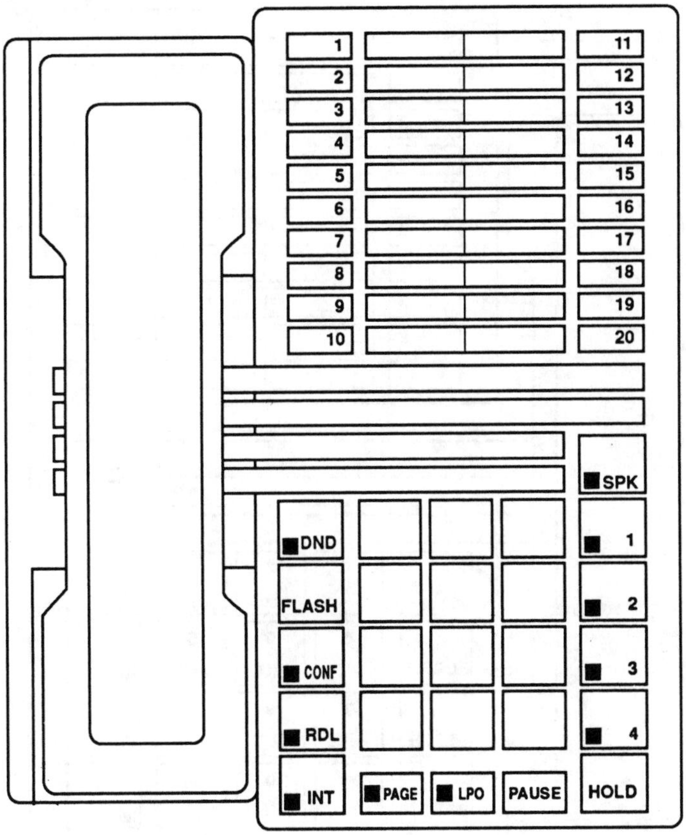

Referring to the exercise you completed a few moments ago, the vast majority of people who attempt it fail to fill in the missing numbers, letters, and characters/symbols accurately (see Figure 2). It is interesting that we use the telephone so often and have done so for many years. Shouldn't we know it better? Maybe we thought that we knew it a lot better than we actually do. If such is the case, that might reflect the "arrogance" of management and portends unfortunate consequences. Truly, "Pride goeth before destruction, and an haughty spirit before a fall."

FIGURE 2 SOLUTION TO EXERCISE

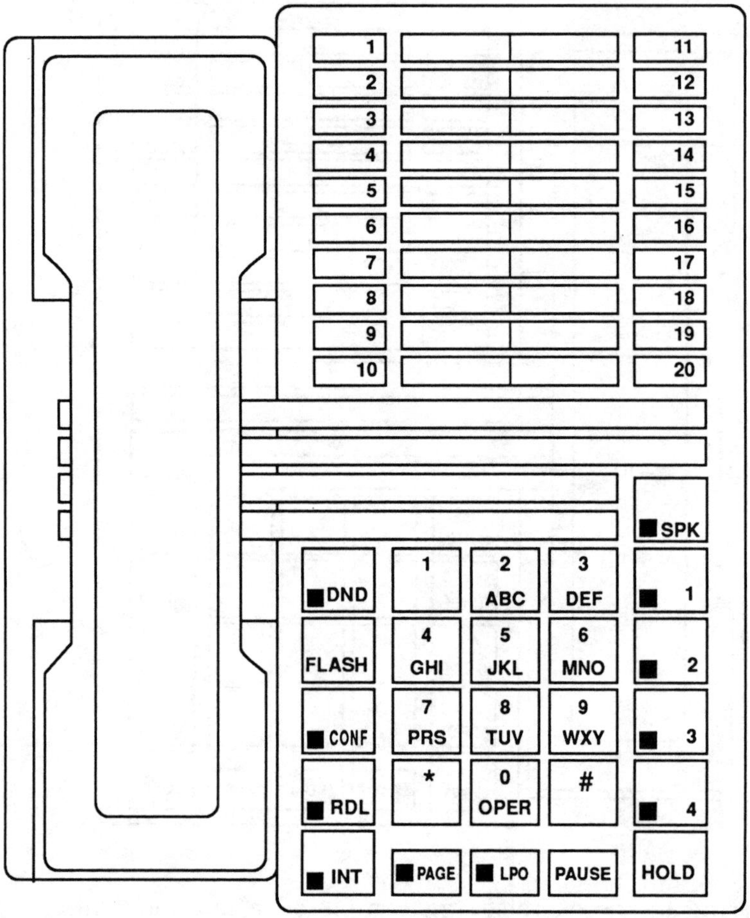

1			11
2			12
3			13
4			14
5			15
6			16
7			17
8			18
9			19
10			20

SPK

DND	1	2 ABC	3 DEF	1
FLASH	4 GHI	5 JKL	6 MNO	2
CONF	7 PRS	8 TUV	9 WXY	3
RDL	*	0 OPER	#	4
INT	PAGE	LPO	PAUSE	HOLD

Enlightened executives examine and continually reexamine their assumptions and standard operating procedures. Self-appraisal and improvement should, therefore, be regarded as ongoing processes. The enhanced sense of self-awareness that usually comes to those who deliberately work toward this end is closely related to self-actualization, not only in terms of professional growth, but in terms of personal growth, as well.

Now That You Have Completed This Program . . .

Congratulations! You have completed the academic curriculum of this program! At the end of just about every MBA in a Nutshell® class that I teach, I notice an interesting and widespread phenomenon: Students feel exhausted by the intensity of the experience yet exhilarated by the realization that they have absorbed so much valuable information in such a short period of time. Invariably, some student poses the following question to me as we prepare to conclude:

"Is that all there is to an MBA?"

The answer is both "Yes" and "No."
Yes.
You have been introduced to key concepts and methods that MBAs commonly use, but you've done it in only a matter of hours. And, I trust, it wasn't painful and might have been enjoyable.
No.
You may wish to learn more about some or many of the subjects covered in *The 12-Hour MBA Program.* At the end of each chapter, a bibliography is provided to suggest supplemental readings. Organizations to support your development in each functional area are also listed there. If your interest in the content of this book is strong enough, you may actually decide to pursue an MBA degree. In that case, you will be able to enjoy the camaraderie of other students and the rich experience of group learning. You also stand to gain a great deal from private and informal conversations with some of your professors.

In any event, your education will still not be complete—not because the MBA curriculum is lacking, but because education is a continuous and ongoing process. I have earned a doctorate as well as an MBA.

Yet I feel the strong desire, if not the need, to read journal articles and thought-provoking books as well as attend seminars as my schedule permits. (Keep in mind that professionals, such as physicians, lawyers, and accountants, are required to be recertified periodically and must study to keep up with professional standards.) I believe that the best of students are eventually struck by the fact that there is always so much more to learn.

RECOMMENDED READING

Carse, James P., *Finite and Infinite Games* (New York: Ballantine Books, 1986).

Kuhn, Thomas S., *The Structure of Scientific Revolutions* (Chicago: University of Chicago Press, 1970).

Minsky, Marvin, *The Society of Mind* (New York: Simon & Schuster, 1985).

Osborn, Alex, *Applied Imagination* (New York: Scribners, 1963).

Patton, Michael Quinn, *Creative Evaluation* (Newbury Park, CA: Sage Publications, 1987).

ORGANIZATIONS AND RESOURCES

Aspen Institute
Carmichael Road, Wye Center
P.O. Box 222
Queenstown, MD 21658
(410) 820-5461

Center for Creative Leadership
P.O. Box 26300
Greensboro, NC 27438-6300
(919) 288-7210

Esalen Institute
Big Sur, CA 93920
(408) 667-3000

National Training Laboratories
1240 N. Pitt Street, Suite 100
Alexandria, VA 22314-1403
(800) 777-LABS

BIBLIOGRAPHY

Aaker, David. *Developing Business Strategies.* New York: John Wiley and Sons, 1984.

Ammer, Christine, and Dean S. Ammer. *Dictionary of Business and Economics.* New York: The Free Press, 1984.

Baumol, William J., and Alan S. Blinder. *Economics: Principles and Policy.* New York: Harcourt Brace Jovanovich, 1991.

Berey, L., and R. Pollay. "The Influencing Role of the Child in Family Decision Making," *Journal of Marketing Research* (February 1986).

Bolman, L. G., and T. E. Deal. *Modern Approaches to Understanding and Managing Organizations.* San Francisco: Jossey-Bass, 1984.

Brabb, George J. *Introduction to Quantitative Management.* New York: Holt Rinehart and Winston, 1968.

Browne, Malcolm W. "Coin-Tossing Computers Found to Show Subtle Bias," *The New York Times*, January 12, 1993.

Byron, Christopher M. *The Fanciest Dive.* New York: W. W. Norton, 1983.

Carbonneau, Thomas. *Alternative Dispute Resolution.* Urbana: University of Illinois Press, 1985.

Casler, Stephen D. *Introduction to Economics.* New York: HarperCollins, 1992.

Cook, Thomas M., and Robert A. Russell. *Introduction to Management Science.* Englewood Cliffs, NJ: Prentice Hall, 1977.

Cooper, W. W., and Yuri Ijiri (eds.). *Kohler's Dictionary for Accountants.* Englewood Cliffs, NJ: Prentice Hall, 1983.

Crosby, Philip. *Let's Talk Quality.* New York: McGraw-Hill, 1989.

Davis, Stan, and Bill Davidson. *2020 Vision.* New York: Simon & Schuster, 1991.

Deming, W. Edwards. *Quality, Productivity, and Competitive Position.* Cambridge, MA: Massachusetts Institute of Technology, 1982.

Downs, Robert B. *Books That Changed the World.* New York: New American Library, 1983.

Evered, James F. *Shirt-Sleeves Management.* New York: AMACOM, 1981.

Festinger, Leon. *A Theory of Cognitive Dissonance.* Evanston, IL: Row Peterson, 1957.

Fulghum, Robert. *All I Really Need to Know I Learned in Kindergarten.* New York: Villard Books, 1988.

Garrett, Thomas M., and Richard J. Klonoski. *Business Ethics,* 2nd ed. Englewood Cliffs, NJ: Prentice Hall, 1986.

Hunninger, E. (ed.). *The Arthur Young Manager's Handbook.* New York: Crown, 1986.

Juran, Joseph M. *Juran's Quality Control Handbook* 4th ed. New York: McGraw-Hill, 1988.

Kotler, Philip. *Marketing Management.* Englewood Cliffs, NJ: Prentice Hall, 1984.

Lawrence, P., and J. Lorsch. *Organization and Environment.* Cambridge, MA: Harvard Business School, Division of Research, 1967.

Lee, Susan. *Susan Lee's ABZs of Economics*. New York: Pocket Books, 1987.

Maslow, Abraham. *Motivation and Personality*. New York: Harper & Row, 1970.

McDonald, John. *Strategy in Poker, Business & War*. New York: W. W. Norton, 1989.

Monger, Rod F. *Mastering Technology*. New York: The Free Press, 1988.

McGregor, D. *The Human Side of Enterprise*. New York: McGraw-Hill, 1960.

Nadler, Leonard. *Designing Training Programs*. Reading, MA: Addison-Wesley, 1982.

Ouchi, William. *Theory Z*. Reading, MA: Addison-Wesley, 1981.

Pava, Calvin. *Managing New Office Technology: An Organizational Strategy*. New York: The Free Press, 1983.

Peters, Tom. *Liberation Management*. New York: Alfred A. Knopf, 1992.

Popcorn, Faith. *The Popcorn Report*. New York: Doubleday, 1991.

Rogers, David J. *Waging Business Warfare*. New York: Kensington, 1987.

Saltus, Richard. "Waiting—Scientists Have a Name for It: Queue Management," *Orange County Register*, November 1, 1992.

Serwer, Andrew. "Patagonia CEO Reels Company In," *Fortune*, December 14, 1992.

Shingo, Shideo. *A Study of the Toyota Production System*. Cambridge, MA: Productivity Press, 1989.

Sobel, Milo. *The Secrets of Professionalism*. New York: The Coronet Consulting Group, 1986.

Stewart, J. D. *The Power of People Skills*. New York: John Wiley and Sons, 1986.

Taha, Hamdy A. *Operations Research*. New York: Macmillan, 1976.

Tyran, Michael R. *The Vest-Pocket Guide to Business Ratios*. Englewood Cliffs, NJ: Prentice Hall, 1992.

Wiener, D., and N. Glaskowsky. *Theory and Problems of Business Law*. New York: McGraw-Hill, 1985.

INDEX